THE WEST IN CRISIS: CIVILIZATIONS AND THEIR DEATH DRIVES

D1521994

The West in Crisis: Civilizations and Their Death Drives

Print Version ISBN: 9798582789291

TABLE OF CONTENTS

About the Author
What Others Have Said

PART I: ATROPOS

Subversion from Within

Atropos: Civilizational Death Drive

PART II: ATROPOS IN ACTION

Preliminaries

A Walk in Prague: Contemplating the West's Achievement

The Real Target of 'Anti-Racism' Protests: Western Civilization and its Values

The Myth of Systemic Racism: In America Reverse Discrimination Is the Norm

Loathing the West: The Real Reason Why "Anti-Racism" Protestors Desecrate Christian Churches

The Aim of Social Justice Movement is Subversion of Core Western Values

What Motivates America's Revolutionists?

The Left's Wonderland: Twilight Zone USA

Democrats' Day of Infamy: The Pernicious Influence of Multiculturalism

Truth about America: Why We are Not a Racist Nation

The Truth about the West: It's the Only Non-Oppressive Civilization

Love of Ancestors and American History

About those Dead White and Black Males

The Left's Way: Violence, Fraud and Intimidation

Black Privilege

Hitler and the Democrats: Leftwing Kindred

Atropic Kin: The Progressive Left Holds the Same Values as Tyrants and Oppressors of the Past

The Political Spectrum: The Correct Delineation

Red Alert: A Revolution in Progress in the USA

This is a Marxist Revolution

Stopping the Revolution: Restore Law and Order

Calling Chomsky Out: The Riots Are A Full-Fledged Attack by The Hard Left to Topple American Society

Utopia Envisioned: Welcome to the Socialist States of Amerika

Leftists Must Not be Allowed to Get Away with Their Criminal Election Fraud

Michael Moore Admits: The Left Will Attempt a Coup

About Those 'Peaceful' Protests: Michelle Obama and the Devious Left

To Katka

ABOUT THE AUTHOR

Vasko Kohlmayer was born and grew up in former communist Czechoslovakia. His writings have appeared in a number of internet and print outlets. They include LewRockwell.com, American Thinker, Human Events, Frontpagemag, The Washington Times, RealClearPolitics, The New York Post, The Baltimore Sun, The Austin-American Statesman and Canada Free Press among others. He can be contacted at vasko.kohlmayer@gmail.com.

WHAT OTHERS HAVE SAID

Vasko Kohlmayer is one of the best writers on social issues today.
— Lew Rockwell, founder of the Mises Institute, editor of LewRockwell.com

Vasko Kohlmayer is one of the finest writers in the conservative/libertarian movement. He is intelligent, courageous, thoughtful, thorough, and most importantly, right.
— Andresen Blom, Washington Editor, *The Economic Standard*

This book is a must read for understanding the current situation in the USA (and in the Western world in general). Read it to find out the name of the evil force behind the riots of the summer of 2020 — the force which has targets far beyond street vandalism and destruction of property.
— Professor Andrew Gorlin

An incredible book that every American needs to read!
— K.S., California

PART I: ATROPOS

SUBVERSION FROM WITHIN

It was in the 1960s that the left convinced itself that there is something fascistic about patriotism and something perversely "patriotic" about running down America. Anti-Americanism - a stand-in for hatred of Western civilization - became the stuff of sophisticates and intellectuals as never before.
— Jonah Goldberg

What is called Western Civilization is in an advanced state of decomposition, and another Dark Ages will soon be upon us, if, indeed, it has not already begun. With the Media, especially television, governing all our lives, as they indubitably do, it is easily imaginable that this might happen without our noticing... by accustoming us to the gradual deterioration of our values.
— Malcom Muggeridge

There is no question that by nearly any metric the West is by far the most successful civilization in history. Among its many spectacular accomplishments, the West has attained affluence and material prosperity that were previously unimaginable. Its scientific advancements and technological progress seem like the stuff of science fiction. Its military power and strength are without equal. But not only do Westerners enjoy unprecedented degree of wealth, health and security, they are also guaranteed unequalled personal liberties and political rights. In short, the West has achieved what those who lived in other civilizations could only dream of. The affluence, freedoms and safety available to Westerners are by any historical measure beyond extraordinary. One clear present-day indicator of the West's staggering success is the countless people from all over the globe willing to take great risks and pay almost any price to come and live here.

All of this notwithstanding, there is an ominous feeling, however, that we are a civilization whose days are numbered. Despite our immense wealth, technological capabilities and military power, there is a growing sense that the West is under an attack it may not be able to withstand.

This attack has not been unleashed by some powerful external enemy. Nor could it have been since no external foe is strong enough to take on this civilization. The attack has come from within. Neither was it launched suddenly. Rather it has been a progressive operation. Low- level and barely perceivable in the beginning, it has been gathering in strength over a period of decades. Its initial phase could be compared to a partisan campaign with a shot taken here and there. Emboldened by a lack of proper response on the part of those it sought to subvert, the enemy expanded its field of hostilities and achieved surprising victories. Invigorated and encouraged by the gains, the foe has recently thrown away all of its disguises and has come out into the open in full force. It has shown itself stronger than most would have imagined with the result that we are now locked in an all-out battle for survival. It is an indication of our malaise that many people are still not fully aware of this.

The enemy ranks are made up of those who harbor an aversion toward their own culture and society. Of those there are many, their numbers stoked up by decades of systematic anti-western indoctrination by the schools and the media. Charging Western civilization with oppression and racism, they claim that our socio-economic system is inherently unjust. Western style liberal democracies, they allege, discriminate and exploit racial minorities, women, homosexuals, transexuals, non-binary people, multi-gender persons, cross-genders and – apart from the select elite chosen from white males – everyone else who happens to abide in the west.

Their allegations, however, are not borne out by facts. As it happens, the West was the first civilization that accorded equal rights to all those within its realms and is the only one that does so consistently. Not only does the West take special care to protect its minorities, it affords them special rights and privileges. This applies to minorities across the spectrum and encompasses race, gender, sexual orientation and whatever other minority criterion exists or may yet be discovered by the progressive illuminati. It is revealing that hundreds of millions of members of minority groups from outside the Western domain are eager to leave their own countries and come to live among us. So much so that if we did not have barriers to hold them back, we would be overrun and that in short order. If we were such an unjust and oppressive civilization as it is claimed, this situation would surely not have arisen.

But facts do not seem to make much difference to these civilizational malcontents. Driven by frustration and anger that are out of kilter with reality, they do not confine themselves to mere verbal critiques but seek to translate their feelings into action. They do this by maligning and undermining the values, beliefs and institutions that have made this civilization what it is. The decades of their persistent efforts have borne fruit. Having been subjected to years of denigration and criticism, Westerners have lost confidence in the fundamental probity of their own culture. Wholesome qualities that once propelled the West to greatness – such as self-denial, deferred gratification, thrift, independence, faithfulness, devotion, etc. – are now commonly ridiculed and despised. They have been increasingly supplanted by such insalubrious tendencies as self-indulgence, pleasure seeking, victim-playing, promiscuity, vulgarity and profligacy. Because the West's cultural and moral foundations have been undermined, the institutions they support cannot but malfunction. Schools, for instance, now routinely teach young people destructive and immoral ideas. Most importantly, they have been for years inculcating students with abhorrence for their own cultural heritage. At the same time the unceasing barrage of decadent propaganda has loosened the bonds of the nuclear family with the result that co-habitation, divorce and out of wedlock births have increased at alarming rates. Because of the general acceptance of profligacy and lack of restraint, western currencies have been steadily losing their purchasing power due to unsustainable levels of debt incurred throughout all layers of our financial system. We could go on but let us say for now that nearly all Western institutions have been – to one degree or another – impaired and marked by decline.

As a consequence of this – and because the West has lost faith in itself – we now stand as a fragile and weakened civilization. This situation has been brought about two complementary courses of action: the long-term efforts of civilizational saboteurs and the failure of the rest to protect their culture, institutions and heritage.

Emboldened by their societies' weakness and apathy, these saboteurs feel that their final goal may be in sight. We have seen a dramatic eruption of their destructive enthusiasm in the late spring and summer of this year when they came out in force under the guise of anti-racism protests. The term saboteur does not, of course, only encompass the vandals wreaking havoc in the streets but also their enablers and protectors in the media, government, transnational organizations, academia and other institutions. In the course of this year, we watched as these players spewed a steady stream of fiery condemnations of western societies as being irredeemably racist, discriminatory and otherwise oppressive. This was naturally accompanied by calls for a radical remaking of our socio-economic model communicated through the catch phrases such as the "The Great Reset," "The New World Order" and "The Fourth Industrial Revolution."

Even as it has attained unprecedented levels of wealth, technological advancement and power, Western civilization finds itself today in an existential crisis and at a point of mortal danger. It is a great irony that the civilization that has provided its people with more affluence, comfort, security, freedom and rights than any other is in danger of being destroyed from within by malcontents that it itself nurtured.

"Know your enemy" said Sun Tzu in his *Art of War*. The great question, then, is this: what motivates these domestic subversives to act in this way? What is the source of the psychological impulses that make them hate and strike against their own societies which – although not perfect – nevertheless belong to the most equitable and humane civilizational stream that has emerged from the currents of history?

This we must understand if we hope to hold back and repulse the insidious forces that threaten the survival of what is left of Western civilization. And this is the question we shall attempt to answer in the pages that follow.

ATROPOS: CIVILIZATIONAL DEATH DRIVE

If it's ours, reject it.
— Sir Roger Scruton on the attitude of European elites

I n his books and writings Sigmund Freud spoke of two drives that actuate the behavior of individual human beings. The first is the drive toward life, propagation and expansion, which manifests itself through sexual instinct. Freud called this drive Eros. The second drive tends toward death and destruction. It manifests itself in behaviors such as aggression and self-harm. This drive has been called Thanatos.

From our study of history and contemporary events we discern and posit the existence of a death drive that runs through whole societies. This civilizational death drive exists as a transpersonal force – a collective psychological vibration – which effectuates the subversion and destruction of societies from which it arises.

We name this civilizational death drive *Atropos*.

In the pages that follow we will show that the dramatic events that began unfolding in the late spring of 2020 in the United States and spread across the Atlantic represented an eruption of this civilizational death drive. Before we apply the concept Atropos to the analysis of the contemporary scene, however, we will make some general observations about its origin and the way it operates.

This drive owes its existence to the psychological energies of people who come to believe that the unhappiness they experience in their lives is the fault of the society in which they live. Believing that the system is somehow responsible for their personal pain and misery, they instinctively become bitter, angry and resentful toward it. As the perceived cause of their suffering, society becomes the object of their dislike and hatred. This feeling naturally gives rise to an urge to take action against it. The psychological motive behind this impulse varies from the wish to exact revenge to the desire to eliminate the source of one's torment. The action can take various forms. It ranges from crude physical violence against societal symbols to formulating sophisticated arguments that seek to delegitimize the values and institutions that have made one's society what it is.

It is the cumulative vibration given off by those who share in this state of mind that supplies Atropos with its energy. Because of its origin, this energy is characterized by frustration, anger and destructiveness. The energetic field of Atropos, however, is not just the sum total of individual vibrations. Once it reaches a certain level of saturation, it starts moving and acting, as it were, on its own. The metaphor of a cloud can help us understand this process. In the initial stages of its formation, a cloud is closely connected with and physically dependent on the climatic conditions of the specific geographic location from which it draws its moisture. However, once it reaches a certain size and density, it becomes detached from its place of origin and floats around seemingly of its own accord. It becomes an independent force, so to speak, that can potentially cause atmospheric disturbance and storms at other locations and in ways that could not have been originally foreseen.

And so it is with Atropos. Once it is sufficiently charged with individual discontent and frustrations, it acquires a life of its own. When this happens, it can eventually discharge its destructive energies in ways that cause profound societal disruption and upheaval. The violent storms then unleashed have potentially the power to sweep away everything in their path. They may even bring down whole civilizations in a kind of civic hurricane.

Even though the strength and potency of Atropos varies and fluctuates depending on many factors and conditions, its existence is intrinsic to the collective psyche of every society. This is because suffering and unhappiness are inherent features of the human condition and a certain portion of the population will always come to blame the system for their suffering and thus supply Atropos with its psychic fuel. Like a black rainbow, then, Atropos hovers over the horizons of societal psychic landscapes. It comes into existence because of a misunderstanding in the human psyche: the Atropic error is essentially one of misplaced blame.

Atropos carries its work of subversion through various individuals and groups. These are the people whose social activities are fueled and motivated by resentment of their society and whose goal is to radically change or completely subvert the system in which they live. These people constitute the army of Atropos. Those in service of Atropos pursue their mission on both the intellectual and practical levels. As to the former, they spread and propagate ideas contrary to the fundamental beliefs and values of their culture. On the practical level, they take actions that weaken and undermine the institutions and ways of doing things which have made their society what it is.

The army of Atropos is diverse and varied. Its members can be found in all walks of life. In our society, they range all the way from university professors through media personalities and politicians to the vandals in the streets. Even though their backgrounds and skills vary considerably, they all work jointly toward a common goal – the subversion of their society. The riots of 2020 revealed the synergetic effectiveness of their cooperation. Sophisticated intellectuals had long prepared the ground by devising arguments purporting to demonstrate the immorality of their culture, claiming that it is, among other evils, intrinsically racist, oppressive and discriminatory. Teachers on all levels of the educational system had used these arguments to indoctrinate several generations of students against the West. When Atropic energy erupted in a violent outpouring in Minneapolis in May of 2020, the Atropos' media squads would both egg on and cover for the vandals who were carrying the work of demolition. At the same time Atropic politicians did their best to facilitate the ruination of their society by tying the hands of law enforcement to prevent them from being able to keep order. In a textbook example of value inversion, Atropic operatives managed to paint America's law enforcement as some immoral enterprise while the criminals and murderers who terrorized the frightened populace were portrayed as noble heroes in the cause of social justice.

The most obvious and distilled manifestation of Western Atropos is the Culture of Repudiation, which has made deep inroads in academia, media and government. The Repudiation Culture can be described as a rejection of fundamental Western values, mores and institutions. Its nature was perhaps best captured by the late Sir Roger Scruton who summed up its ethos as: "Whatever is ours, reject it." The Culture of Repudiation is a direct attack on the very underpinnings of our civilization. A civilization that rejects its culture rejects itself and as such cannot survive for very long. The Culture of Repudiation thus represents an attempt at civilizational suicide by cultural self-abnegation. Proponents of this movement are well aware of this, which is the very reason they propagate it.

Multiculturalism, especially its hardcore varieties, is another expression of Atropos. Like the practitioners of the Culture of Repudiation, hardcore western multiculturalists are actuated by a strong animus toward their own heritage. They invariably put down and belittle their culture while extolling the purported virtues of foreign and exotic ones. They seek to subvert their society by dilution on both the intellectual and practical levels by importing beliefs, values and practices that are contrary to those which make the functioning of their own society possible. Advocacy of unrestricted immigration, especially from the parts of the world whose cultural values are removed from our own, is a practical expression of the Atropic multicultural mindset. The objective of such policies is obvious: to dilute native societies with foreign elements to the point they cease to be recognizable in their traditional form. In a number of Western nations this task has been largely accomplished.

The social justice movement is another means through which Atropos carries on its work of subversion. Comprised of various seemingly unrelated groups and factions with apparently differing agendas, they all share their animus toward the Western system. Even though they all seem to come from different starting points and purport to represent different demographics, they are all rooted in that identical mindset and propagate the same underlying narrative. They all condemn Western societies as inherently immoral, because they allegedly discriminate against and oppress various groups. Such claims reveal the true nature of the social justice movement, because they are obviously false. The truth is that societies spawned by the Western civilizational stream are the only ones that guarantee equal rights to all people and groups living within their confines. The incongruence between their rhetoric and reality shows what the true goal of the social justice movement is. It is decidedly not to help the alleged "victims" of non-existent oppression, but to radically alter the nature of their society by adopting policies that would make it impossible for it to operate in its present form.

The advocacy and promotion of sexual aberrations such as male and female homosexuality, transsexuality and various types of gender distortion is another means through which Atropos carries out its work of societal dissolution. For most people who become entrapped in these deviancies it becomes nearly impossible to hold traditional western values given that their behavior runs in direct contravention of them. Because of the physically and psychologically destabilizing effects of these lifestyles on the human person, such people can rarely function as stable pillars of their communities. Thus, society as a whole is weakened.

Championing Marxism and its ideological offshoots is another evidence of the Atropic sensibility. This is because the socialist approach – with its centralization of state power which inevitably brings about oppression of various kinds – is diametrically opposed to the western evolution toward individual freedom and liberties. Socialism and Western liberalism represent two irreconcilable worldviews that are inimical to each other. Importation of socialist values and ways fundamentally undermines the principles on which western type societies are based.

Atropos and the Political Left

For the last one hundred and fifty years or so the troops of Atropos would congregate and mobilize on the political left. This is not to say that the whole of the left has been co-opted by the civilizational death drive. The portion of the left that has been in service of Atropos is what has been called the hard or radical left. Today the hard left encompasses many factions. It includes, among others, those who are commonly referred to as progressives and the woke.

The type of people and groups that occupy the hard left change over time. Up to the first half of the 20th century, the hard left was dominated primarily by Marxist-style revolutionists and card-carrying communists. Today the hard left is mostly comprised of Critical Theory ideologues, Antifa and BLM type zealots and various elements of the social justice movement such anti-racism warriors, feminists, homosexual rights activists, transexual activists and such. But even though the elements of the hard left keep changing with time and their language may superficially differ, their frame of mind remains identical: they all harbor profound animus toward Western type societies which they contend are immoral and irredeemably flawed.

Actuated by the energies of Atropos, the hard left's ultimate goal has always been the same: to do away with the "system." Not all of them always express their mission in such blunt terms, but it is clear that this is, in fact, their objective. Radical leftists often speak of reforming their societies, but when we examine the measures they advocate, their proposals are invariably so drastic that they would change the society to the point where it would effectually cease to be what it is. The purpose of this particular approach is to effect societal destruction under the guises of reform rather than by direct revolution.

The destructive impulse of the hard left came to a full view during the so-called George Floyd protests of 2020. After the protests got into full swing, the instigators and organizers largely dropped their pretense of fighting for racial justice and become quite open about the fact that their goal was the overthrow of society. To make their aim obvious, they targeted symbols of Western culture such as the statues of men who made contributions to its advancement. They also attacked churches which are a physical reminder of the fact that Christianity is one of the two main pillars of the Western civilization. On many of the structures they desecrated the protesters drew anarchist and pagan graffiti, thus making their agenda and goals as explicit as they possibly could. The immediate goal of their rioting was to wreak maximal havoc and anarchy in order to destabilize and topple the present system. The pagan signs they left behind show a desire for a completely new order of things, based on principles that stand in direct opposition to the western way.

The vandals, arsonists and desecrators who wrought havoc throughout the Western world functioned as demolition squads of Atropos, the civilizational death drive. They were cheered on and protected by their compadres in the media, the Democrat Party, academia and the courts, among other places. Working in concert toward the same goal, their combined efforts brought the system to the brink. At the beginning of the 3rd decade of the 21st century Atropos is waxing strong and Western civilization finds itself in great peril. Standing on the edge of a precipice civilizational death is an imminent possibility.

After nearly six decades of persistent and systematic efforts the radicals have made western societies ready for capture. The mass of western peoples is simply unable to effectively defend their civilizational inheritance, because they have been left demoralized and confused by the years of relentless propaganda and attacks. The key institutions throughout the West – such as the judiciary, education, media, and government bureaucracies – have been infiltrated by Atropic operatives who weakened them to the point that they do not perform their intended function.

Thus, when in late spring of 2020 things reached the boiling point in the crisis-ridden West, the Hard Left seized the opportunity to pounce. As the West's standard bearer, the United States became the site of the initial Atropic eruption. Falsely claiming that America was an irredeemably racist and oppressive nation, the Left attacked it with fury and vengeance. After decades of brainwashing and cultural weakening, Americans were unequipped to stand up to the specious assault. It took many days for anyone to clearly point out the obvious fact that rather than being oppressed, American blacks are the most cosseted and advantaged minority in history, one that enjoys unprecedented privileges and opportunities. Facts notwithstanding, the Atropic revolutionaries were able to seize the high moral ground and were allowed to unleash violence which came to be seen as the justifiable means of bringing about "social justice."

With law enforcement vilified and hamstrung, anarchy and lawlessness prevailed in many places across America. Portland and Seattle were two prime examples. The chaos there was explicitly encouraged by local Atropic politicians. In an interview with CNN, a far-left partisan called Jenny Durkan, who at the time served as Mayor of Seattle, brushed away any suggestion of federal assistance to help to quell the disorder that had engulfed her city. Instead, she claimed that this was just a peaceful movement, a type of "block party" which was possibly going to usher another "summer of love." The predictably calamitous string of events that took place after she had made this reality-denying comment clearly exposed her as being part of the Atropic enterprise.

Being actuated by dark energies of frustration, anger and hatred, the fruits of Atropos are death, terror and destruction. Thus, every single successful hard leftist coup has spawned systems where mass murder and general ruination became the norm. Just ask the people of the Soviet Union, People's Democratic Republic of Germany, Mao's China, Castro's Cuba, Hitler's Third Reich, North Korea or any other country where the Hard Left managed to seize power. Whenever it reigns supreme, Atropos leaves in its wake ashes, graves and ruins. Heartless and cruel, Atropos browbeats and demoralizes the unfortunate populations by stripping them of their freedoms, rights and dignity. Never delivering on its promises of paradisical utopia that its adherents envision, Atropos creates hell on earth. Terrible indeed are the works of this dark force.

PART II: ATROPOS IN ACTION

Death Drive Observed

PRELIMINARIES

Truth has to be repeated constantly, because Error also is being preached all the time, and not just by a few, but by the multitude.
— Johann Wolfgang von Goethe

As we pointed out above, the West's civilizational death drive – Atropos – carries out its work of societal destruction through the political left. To put it in a different way, the hard left is the means through which Atropos effects its work of societal subversion.

Being in the thrall of Atropos, the left's psychological stance is inherently anti-western. This means that the left's activities are motivated and actuated by its animus toward the values and ways underpinning Western civilization. Driven by its antipathy to it, the left's final objective is nothing less than the vitiation of this socio-political system.

This fact is not always easy to discern, since most of the time evidence of the Atropic animus is not readily obvious. Nor is it openly admitted by most of those who harbor it. It is especially difficult to detect by observers who are not aware of its existence in the first place. To conceal their true motives, those on the left have consistently claimed that their deeds are inspired by love, compassion and other such noble motives. Many well-meaning people either believe such claims or at least give them the benefit of the doubt. They do not carefully analyze the left's actions and thus fail to recognize their corrosive effect on their society and civilization at large. What makes it difficult for unsuspecting people to see the truth is their inability to imagine that the activities some of their fellow citizens could be fueled by hatred of their own culture and community. Then there are those who sense that something is not quite right, but they lack the intellectual framework to properly grasp or articulate what may be wrong with leftists and their works.

Only a relatively small sliver of the left is honest about their true feelings and goals. There are few who openly confess their aversion to the Western way of life and their desire to do away with societies that practice it. These honest elements, however, are usually seen only as an extremist minority residing on the far fringe of the spectrum. But this is not the case. The haters of the West do not constitute merely some small clique on the left. They are only more sincere than their ideological compadres who disingenuously conceal their aversion toward western ways under the false façade of love, compassion, tolerance and such. The truth of their motives is actually the opposite of their claims.

Note: not all those on the left are driven by active hatred of their Western heritage. There are some individuals who get involved with leftist causes because they have been deceived, or they are confused, or they want to appear to be good and caring people. In other words, they fall into the category Lenin used to call "useful idiots."

In the spring of 2020 something portentous happened. The Atropic energy which had been building up in the left's collective psyche for decades, mostly under the surface and unnoticed by most, suddenly erupted with great force. The trigger was the death of George Floyd in Minneapolis during his arrest on May 25. The incident broke the sluice gate lock, as it were, and the accumulated reservoir of Atropic energy began gushing through the left's entrails in one great stream.

Sensing blood and supercharged with the overflow of destructive spirit, the left sprang into action. Having perceived weakness in our troubled, crisis-ridden civilization, the left threw away the gloves and went for the jugular. Baring its teeth and moving in for the kill, it dropped its mask of goodness to reveal its ugly face. Suddenly it became all too obvious that the left is neither kind, nor loving, nor tolerant, nor inclusive. Now everyone with the eyes to see could recognize that, rather than being caring and compassionate, the left is actually violent, destructive, hateful, oppressive, angry, censorious and intolerant. In addition, the latest election also exposed leftists as consummate fraudsters and cheats. What also became very clear was that these qualities do not only define the fringes but run all the way through the left's core and center. They were on ample display all across the field – from the hoodlums on the streets, through suave media figures like Anderson Cooper to powerful politicians like Kamala Harris. And all in between. In the process we witnessed billionaire owners of social media platforms overseeing brazen forms of censorship while sophisticated intellectuals kept churning out blatant lies about the nature of this deleterious movement.

Weakened societies are almost invariably brought down by violence. Thus it was that violence became the focus and the centerpiece of the left's efforts the moment it erupted with such force in late May. The left correctly perceived that in order to achieve its objective of societal subversion, the violence had to be intensified and prolonged for as long as possible. Consequently, all the elements of the left's juggernaut began working in concord toward this goal. To begin with, it was imperative that regular citizens not become fully aware of the extent of the violence and the damage it was causing. The idea was to keep concerned Americans from rising up and demanding the end of it by putting pressure on politicians and law enforcement. It was for this purpose that the mainstream media kept describing the riots as "the mostly peaceful protests" and carefully avoided broadcasting footage of devastation and mayhem. Even as America was being torn apart by the most violent social upheaval in its history – which the insurance industry declared "a catastrophe" across multiple states – many people had no real idea of what was happening, thanks to the successful conceal-ment efforts of the mainstream media outlets.

The media was deftly seconded by leftist intellectuals who provided both justification and cover. Among the many ex-amples we could list, we just mention the world-renowned aca-demic Noam Chomsky who managed to utter the following words with a completely straight face:

> The Black Lives Matter protests which is a huge, in-credible development: the biggest social movement in American history. A huge number of people involved spontaneously, solidarity black and white together, con-structive goals, develop good programs, really great things happening... At the fringes they are people who are breaking windows, intimidating somebody at the restaurant... Things like this shouldn't be happening, but that's not what's going on. What's going on is a mas-sive, non-violent, constructive social movement.[1]

That was a blatant lie by Professor Chomsky. No other move-ment in the history of this country has wrought more damage than the 2020 riots. The only domestic event that has caused more devastation in America was the Civil War.

For their part, leftist politicians on all levels did their best to lend their support and give encouragement to the ransackers who were laying waste to American cities and terrorizing com-munities up and down the country. This they did in two main ways. First, they tied the hands of law enforcement so that law and order would not be restored. In some places they went so far as to accommodate the rioters' demand of defunding the po-lice. Secondly, the politicians would signal to rioters to continue their work and even urge them to step it up further. A notable instance of this was the democratic vice-presidential candidate Kamala Harris who in an online interview with Stephen Colbert spurred the rioters on with these words:

> They're not gonna stop. And that's – they're not – this

is a movement, I'm telling you. They're not gonna stop. And everyone beware, because they're not gonna stop... They're not gonna stop before election day in November, and they're not gonna stop after election day.[2]

To see where leftists really stand, contemplate this fact: as of today, no major figure on the left has either condemned the violence or called for prosecution of those responsible for the injuries, damage and deaths that have occurred as a result of it.

To further their cause, the woke operatives in Big Tech did their part by imposing severe censorship on those who tried to document and expose what was actually taking place. By the summer of 2020 cancel culture reached unprecedented proportions. Conservative posts and their authors were being purged from platforms of public discourse in a systemic manner. Their social media accounts were blocked or cancelled for simply stating the truth. Many of those who objected to the left's methods were harassed, threatened, assaulted, fired from their jobs and had their reputations ruined.

The true nature and goal of the "protest" movement should become clear once we recognize the manifest falsity of its purported cause. Spearheaded by BLM, the riots were cast as a righteous uprising against the systemic racism that allegedly runs rampant in the United States. The problem with this claim is that it is simply not true. The opposite is, in fact, the case. Rather than being a racist country, the United States has made its black people the most advantaged and privileged minority in history. Blacks in America enjoy a whole array of privileges and benefits that are unavailable to the rest of population. Reverse discrimination is a common practice in education, government employment and other areas of life. In the last twelve years America has elected a black president twice and if the initial result of the 2020 presidential election stands, America will have a black vice-president next year. Given the advanced age of Joe Biden – who would be 82 years old at end of his first term – it is quite likely that Kamala Harris will be called upon to ascend to the presidency at some point during his term in office. If this likely scenario does indeed take place, America will have had two black presidents in three out of the last four presidential cycles. Moreover, Harris would also have the honor of being the first female president in the history of the United States. Could anything like this ever happen in a racist country? The truth is that both Barrack Obama and Kamala Harris ascended to the very pinnacle of the American power structure because they are black. Given their modest accomplishments prior to their spectacular rise to the top, they would not get anywhere close to the Oval Office if they were white. The black color of their skin was not an obstacle. Quite to the contrary, it was their advantage and a ticket to success. So much about America being a racist society.

To any sane person it must be obvious that the protest/riot movement that shook America to its core in 2020 was launched and conducted on a fraudulent basis and under false pretenses. Rather than intended to right a non-existent injustice, the allegations of racism were only a cover for an entirely different agenda and goal. The agenda was the destabilization of American society and the goal its overthrow.

We can clearly see the riots' Atropic purpose if we consider the kinds of targets the so-called anti-racist protestors marked for destruction. In the weeks following the death of George Floyd hundreds of attacks against Catholic churches were reported across America. This may seem strange, given that America's woke commissars of social justice never really charged the Catholic Church with complicity in this country's current "racist" regime or Floyd's death. If anything, in recent years the Church has been a notable abettor of the progressive movement, having incorporated parts of the woke agenda into its own teachings. This has been especially true during the pontificate of Francis who in many ways sounds like a secular progressive clad in papal robes.

The protestors' raids on Catholic churches, therefore, bewildered many people. But if you remember what the left's driving impulse is, these acts will make perfect sense. Despite its recent dabbling in wokeness, the Catholic Church – along with our classical Greco-Roman heritage – has been a foundational pillar of Western civilization. This is the real reason why the churches became a target of the left's destructive urge. To make their motivation completely clear, in some instances the protestors even inscribed sickle and hammer on the walls of the sacred structures they vandalized. Sickle and hammer stand, of course, for the Soviet Union and its communist revolution which denounced the western model and established a new system based on ideas that were antithetical to occidental tradition.

The attacks on churches, however, were not the only clue exposing the hidden agenda behind the faux anti-racist protests. The war on statues was just as revealing. They initially began with monuments of those who had at least some connection – however remote or tenuous – to slavery. Very quickly, however, no statue was safe from the mob's wrath. So much so that they targeted even those who had done much for the advancement and liberation of black people. Abraham Lincoln would be one of them. This despite the fact that Lincoln is generally considered to be the man who effectually ended slavery in the United States. The widely-held view of Lincoln as the emancipator of black people was well expressed by the journalist Edward Achorn who wrote recently that in most Americans' eyes Lincoln stands as "a symbol of wisdom, decency, sacrifice, and perseverance in defeating slavery and liberating millions of black Americans."[3]

And yet the allegedly "anti-racism" protesters repeatedly attacked Lincoln's statues across America. The attacks were so flagrant that even CNN had to take notice. In its October 12 dispatch, CNN reported that "protesters in Portland, Oregon, pulled down statues of Abraham Lincoln and Theodore Roosevelt..."

The protesters did not stop there, however. As part of their statue rampage, they also attacked edifices associated with our national heritage. In a piece headlined "The Mob Goes After Abraham Lincoln," the Daily Signal reported that they "trashed the Oregon Historical Society, which preserves treasures of the past so that people of succeeding generations may understand their culture and history."[4]

The next morning CNN quoted Portland Police Chief Chuck Lovell who made this observation: "These events late at night, they purport to have a racial justice nexus. But they're not that. They're about violence and criminal destruction."[5]

Chuck Lovell is absolutely correct. The rioters' actions had nothing to do with race – they were all about destruction. As was the case with the churches, their behavior may seem irrational, but only until we remind ourselves of the fact that the left is the means through which Atropos carries out its work of societal vitiation. The structures and statues the so-called protestors vandalized commemorated the efforts of people who in one way or another advanced the cause of western civilization. It was the protestors' deep-seated antipathy toward the west that explains why they acted the way they did.

Since the Atropic mindset is transnational in nature, we could expect that a powerful eruption of its energies in one country would trigger corresponding disruptions in other countries within the western stream. And this was, in fact, what happened. Within two weeks of the start of the George Floyd riots in the United States, similar events began taking place in other western nations. According to Wikipedia:

> After Floyd's death, protests were held globally against the use of excessive force by police officers against black suspects and lack of police accountability. Protests began in Minneapolis the day after his death and developed in cities throughout all 50 U.S. states and internationally.[6]

The protests waxed especially strong in leading European countries such as the United Kingdom, France and Germany where hundreds of thousands took part. On June 6th a British newspaper ran a report which opened as follows:

> Furious Europeans have taken to the street this week to protest against police brutality and racism, following

the death of George Floyd in the US, as major capitals across the EU were shut down by the protesters. Europeans have defied official bans against mass gatherings across the continent, as protests continue to erupt across major capitals from Paris to Berlin.[7]

The piece continued by listing some of the European nations where the "protests" took place.

Thousands have taken to the streets in Europe to protest racism and police brutality, following the tragic US police killing of George Floyd, which has first triggered a wave of protests in America. Thousands poured in the streets in countries including France, Germany, Spain, Belgium, the Netherlands, Austria, Finland, Slovakia, Greece, Ireland, Poland, Sweden and others.[8]

It is deeply significant that the protests in Europe were organized by chapters of BLM. This should make us pause, given that BLM is an American organization which came into existence in 2013 in response to a shooting death of a black American teenager in Florida. Why, then, is this outfit organizing mass demonstrations across Europe? And even more importantly, why is Black Lives Matter trying to incite protests in countries that have virtually no black populations? In nations such Finland, Poland, Ireland or Slovakia – which are for the most part ethnically homogenous – racism has never been a significant problem.

So, again, the question forces itself: Why would BLM instigate protests in countries that do not really have racial issues? Whatever these protests were about, they could definitely not have been about racism.

This contradiction reveals what BLM is truly after: Black Lives Matter is a revolutionary outfit whose real agenda is the destabilization of western societies through upheaval and violence that invariably accompany its demonstrations, which it disingenuously portrays as events aimed at combating racial injustice.

Founded by militant revolutionaries, BLM is a seditious operation whose ultimate objective is the overthrow of the western socio-economic system. In a 2015 video, BLM co-founder and Board president Patrisse Cullors admitted that she and her colleagues in the leadership are "trained Marxists."[9] And these Marxists are clearly determined to implement their ideology in America and throughout the western world. This is what Cullors wrote in the conclusion of her recent missive to members of her organization: "I know I can speak for most of us. We have fought like hell for our freedom and we will continue to fight like hell."[10]

Given the ideological disposition and attitude of the Black Lives Matter leadership, it was completely predictable that, as had happened in America, the BLM demonstrations in Europe would quickly take a violent turn.

"Black Lives Matter Protests Turn Violent Across Europe"[11] announced a headline from VOA News June 13, barely two weeks after the George Floyd incident in Minneapolis. The article opened as follows: "Riot police fired tear gas and charged at violent protesters at an anti-racism rally in Paris on Saturday..."[12]

The piece then lists various European hotspots where violence took place. In the process we learn that even in normally calm Switzerland adherents of a "leftist group threw objects at police, as a wave of anger continued to sweep the world following the death of African American George Floyd."

In the meantime, things were heating up in London, as conveyed by this headline from Express Online:

London Protests Turn Violent As Police and Demonstrators Clash Outside Downing Street.[13]

The first line of the article read: "A Black Lives Matter protest in London has turned violent this afternoon after police and demonstrators clashed outside Downing Street." It then continued:

While Boris Johnson was inside No. 10, leading the Government's daily coronavirus press briefing, anger was mounting just hundreds of metres away. Officers and a number of demonstrators protesting against police violence following the death of George Floyd in the US have become engulfed in an angry confrontation with a number of objects being thrown.[14]

As is invariably the case anywhere BLM gets involved, the police came under attack. This is part and parcel of a deliberate strategy. Radical leftists can only take over societies if there is a breakdown of law and order. It is then that they can unleash their reign of terror and intimidate the terrified populations into submission. This is why BLM is such an enthusiastic supporter of the "defund the police" movement. "We call for a national defunding of police,"[15] asserts a May 30th post on the BLM website. The title of the declaration which features this onerous demand is "#DefundThePolice."

Here is another UK report from the past summer:

> BLM (Black Lives Matter) protests were attended by thousands across the UK over the weekend, sparking some violent confrontations with police officers, branded 'disgusting' by the Metropolitan Police Federation chairman, Ken Marsh.[16]

The article goes on to speak about Ken Marsh, who is one of Britain's highest-ranking law enforcement officials, and who has apparently not yet completely succumbed to the virus of political correctness that has infected most of western institutions.

> Ken Marsh said he was 'disgusted, sickened, and appalled' by protester violence towards the police at BLM protests across the country. He told Talk Radio: 'I'm not sure what my colleagues have done to warrant this abuse. It's absolutely absurd and wholly unfair.'[17]

Once again, the protesters' actions and statements were rife with contradictions. The most glaring among them was the fact that much of the violence and upheaval was unleashed in the name of George Floyd. Everywhere you looked you could see placards and banners with Floyd's name and image. Consider this description of an incipient riot in London: "Crowds then moved towards No 10 after gathering this afternoon where they chanted Mr Floyd's name."[18]

This prompts a series of questions:

Why would Europeans want to attack their own law enforcement for the death of a man that took place in a country thousands of miles away in an American state they could not even locate on the map? What did the Swiss police have to do with Floyd's demise and why did a Swiss leftist group shower Swiss cops with projectiles?

Why would Europeans blame their own national institutions for an incident that occurred on the other side of the Atlantic? Why did they direct their anger at their own government officials? What exactly was Boris Johnson's connection the demise of George Floyd in Minnesota? How was the British prime minister responsible for the conduct of the officers from the city of Minneapolis' third police precinct? And yet the rioters demanded his resignation and the British police had to reinforce security at his residence to shield him from physical danger.

On the face of it, this does not make logical sense. Not until, that is, we understand that what we saw was a manifestation of the Atropic animus of which the left is the instrument. What the left was trying to do was to unsettle and destabilize western nations, and it used the cover of George Floyd for the purpose.

The parallels on both sides of the Atlantic were striking and show that the behavior of the revolutionists in America and Europe was not only coordinated but sprang from the same psychological root. As happened in the US, the "protestors" in Europe also embarked on a statue-slaying rampage. They first began with those for whom at least a tenuous connection could be made with slavery, but the pretense of racism quickly receded into the background, and soon no statue remained safe. Perhaps most notably, statues of Winston Churchill, the legendary prime minister who led Britain during World War II, came under assault. The situation became so critical that a deeply symbolic Churchill sculpture in the heart of London had to be boarded up to protect it from the BLM mob. One can clearly sense the delight of the *Washington Post* as it reported this development:

LONDON — In the predawn hours Friday, workers boarded up an iconic Winston Churchill statue outside the Palace of Westminster to protect the public art work from further vandalism... Encased now in a large wooden box, painted a dull gray, the monument resembles a shipping crate, or an upright coffin — or the mysterious monolith from Stanley Kubrick's science fiction masterpiece, '2001: A Space Odyssey.'[19]

For his part, Boris Johnson wrote on Twitter that it was "absurd and shameful" that Churchill's monument was in danger of being wrecked. Johnson was, of course, correct, but it is also indicative of the West's malaise that rather than taking tough measures against the perpetrators of these crimes leading politicians limit their actions to expressions of indignation on social media platforms.

But what so enraged the protestors about Winston Churchill? After all, Churchill was neither a slave owner nor did he advocate racial discrimination in Britain. Considered one of the greatest Englishmen who ever lived, he stands as one of the most beloved British politicians of all time. And deservedly so, since it was his exemplary courage and determination that pulled Britain through the dark days of the Second World War. Yet it is precisely there, at the point of his greatest achievement, that we find the explanation for the seemingly senseless attacks again him. Even though most normal people were genuinely shocked and perplexed by this, from the vantage point of the west hating Atropic left the attacks made complete sense. By his fortitude and will, Winston Churchill was instrumental in helping to save Western civilization: first in the face of the evil Nazis and then by taking a strong stand against the equally depraved Soviets. That's why the left hates him so.

The riots that began in the spring of 2020 gave us a unique opportunity to observe Atropos in action. The protests that we witnessed in America and other western countries had nothing to do with racism, because the racism they claimed to oppose simply does not exist. A false cause *par excellence*, racism was merely used by the forces of Atropos as a cover under which to carry out their work of destabilizing and potentially toppling western societies.

It is not often in the history of civilizations that we see Atropos moving in such a powerful and obvious way. Even as I watched transfixed the unfolding civilizational drama of 2020, I was writing articles and essays in which I sought to expose the underlying forces and motives that drove those dramatic events. You can say that I was writing a commentary in real time on the life-and-death Atropic spectacle that was unfolding right before our eyes. I did it in hope of showing my fellow Westerners the real truth and meaning of what was happening in our societies. This I tried to do by bringing to light the Left's true motives and the deleterious role it plays in the civilizational struggle we find ourselves in. I also sought to expose the lies on the back of which the left tries to implement its agenda. Principal among them are the claims that America is a racist nation and that western system is inherently oppressive. Over and over, I pointed out that this is not true. Making the same point repeatedly may seem superfluous, but I felt that the repetition is necessary because these untruths have gained a deep hold in many quarters. Because of this they need to be countered again and again until the light of truth penetrates the minds of those who have been deceived by them. These lies are repeated relentlessly every day and we have to answer them as often as they come if we hope to break their hold. I believe that in the present-day environment when falsehoods come from nearly every corner, it is justifiable and even essential to keep restating the same truths to combat the deception.

The text that follows consist primarily of the writings that I produced as I was trying to make sense of these extraordinary times. I have made some adjustments and expanded the original essays in places for the purpose of this book. It is my earnest prayer and hope that this book will give the public the framework to see the events we have witnessed for what they truly are. We will do well if we see and grasp this point fully: the political left is tool of a destructive transpersonal psychological force that seeks subvert our civilization.

Dramatic and destabilizing Atropic eruptions, such as we have seen in 2020 across the western world, usually occur in weakened civilizations that are nearing the end of their lifecycle. The end, however, is not inevitable. There have been cases in history where crisis-ridden, foundering civilizations reversed course to save themselves and continued to flourish for a long time yet. Rome, for example, went through a deep civilizational crisis in the second half of the first century AD. At that difficult time a selfless, patriotic man by the name of Vespasian,[20] a commoner by birth, rose to the top and by his wisdom and courage extended the lease on life of that great civilization from whose achievements we still benefit today.

It is imperative that we fully grasp the meaning of this year's dramatic events and summon the wisdom to do what needs to be done to save ourselves. The question is: will we find the courage to push back against the west-hating left or will we just stand by as Atropos continues its work of civilizational destruction?

Our destiny and the fate of our civilization is in our hands. It is truly for such a time as this that we have been born. Which way will we go?

A WALK IN PRAGUE: CONTEMPLATING THE WEST'S ACHIEVEMENT

I t was good to visit Prague once again. Known as the "City of a Hundred Spires," it truly is a marvelous place. Positioned in the center of Europe on the banks of the meandering Vltava, it has been long acknowledged to be among the most beautiful cities on the continent. This surely means something, for Europe is home to many stunning cities: Rome, Florence, Athens, Paris, Vienna, Cologne, Venice, Bern. The list goes on…

In almost all of these great cities you can still locate their ancient heart – usually a square – where in times past the elders would come together to confer on the affairs of their community. It was also a point where the people would gather to take part in their civic life. Prague's ancient heart is called the Old Town Square. This stately plaza – in which the mixture of architectural styles bears witness to the wealth of its history – is presided over by the Old Town Hall, a medieval structure built out of large limestone blocks. An imposing watchtower was completed above it in 1364. Standing at nearly seventy meters tall, its peak was the highest point in the city through the medieval age. Crowned with a steeple roof flanked by four turrets, the whole structure is exquisitely balanced. Constructed without the aid of motors or electric tools in an era when most people did not expect to live past the age of forty, the edifice is a testimony to the indomitability of the human soul. By creating something so robust and charming, its builders clearly wanted to leave behind something that would transcend the ephemerality of their personal existence. In this they surely have succeeded. The balance and dignity of their creation take your breath away even centuries after the hands of those who built it had turned to dust. But even though the builders are long gone, they still speak to us through the stone testaments they left behind. Contemplating their handiwork, one cannot but stand in awe of the people whose skill and determination brought an edifice of such grandeur into being.

Incorporated into the south side of the Old City Hall is another triumph of the human spirit: the magnificent Prague Astronomical Clock. The Orloj, as it is also often called, was mounted more than 600 years ago. It has the distinction of being the third oldest clock of its kind built in Europe and the oldest one that is still in service. A marvel of human ingenuousness, it displays, among other things, four different times simultaneously: Central European, Old Bohemian, Babylonian and Celestial.

During the summer the stone pavement under the Clock is normally taken by throngs of tourists who gaze up dumbstruck with wonder. This year, however, the square is much quieter, because of the restrictions imposed on international travel by the coronavirus. But no worldly event or happening can stop time's inexorable flow, which the Orloj keeps tracking ceaselessly. As the legendary Czech singer Karel Gott once sang: "Time's flight is frenzied. I cannot catch it nor can you." A long-time resident of Prague, the singer must have looked many times at the Great Clock as did so many generations of residents before him. Time caught up with Karel Gott last year, as it will with each one of us one day. Of this the Orloj reminds us twenty-four times a day. At the top of every hour, the south side wall of the Old Townhall becomes the host to an extraordinary kinetic spectacle. A skeleton that stands on the Clock's right side pulls a string which sounds a bell. The blue star-covered shutters on the two windows above move sideways, and we see a procession of the twelve apostles – the faithful disciples of Jesus of Nazareth – making their solemn round. Each hour the ancient mechanism unfailingly performs this deeply symbolic pageant. Time and death, ephemerality and transcendence, fragility and resilience, limitation and hope all come into play on the thick walls of that grand old structure. There the complex machinery momentously reenacts the drama of the human condition with a pathos that touches the soul in a way that is difficult to put into words.

About two hundred and fifty meters north of the Clock, on a boulevard called Pařížská Ulice, is an emporium of Patek Philippe. Patek Philippe, a Swiss watch-making company founded in 1832, has its manufacturing facilities in the Vallée de Joux along France's eastern border. Renowned for its beautifully designed timepieces of high complexity, some of Patek's models consist of more than 1,300 individual components. Amazingly, Patek's skilled watchmakers are able to assemble all those parts into miniature machines that fit in a case that is only some four centimeters across and one and a half centimeters thick. These little wonders can simultaneously display seconds, minutes, hours, days of week, date, moon phases, power reserve and a second time zone among other functions. In addition, some models also double up as highly accurate chronographs. Marvels of design, engineering and technology, they bear testimony to their makers' tremendous ingenuity, skill and patience. So great is their technical virtuosity that they make it possible for a person to wear what is in essence a miniature Orloj on one's wrist. These timepieces, however, are not only phenomenal mechanical contraptions, they are also objects of great beauty that testify to the refinement and taste of their creators. A Patek timepiece is always as much a mechanical wonder as it is an object of art.

The Prague Astronomical Clock and the Patek Philippe store are less than three hundred steps from each other. Both of them were brought into existence by the same impulse: the need of a forward-looking, goal-oriented civilization to keep track of time. And they both met that need with great ingenuity and style. But even though the two are very close in terms of physical distance, it took a journey of more than half a millennium to get from one to the other. Patek came out with its ultra-complicated series called the *Grandmaster Chime* in 2014. Its unveiling took place six centuries after the Orloj's inaugural peal announced to the world that its minute hand had completed its first revolution. In that long expanse of time, Western civilization led the world on a path of progress in nearly every area of human endeavor: technology, science, art, commerce, philosophy, politics.

This progress was made possible largely because a historically strange idea gradually took root in the West. The idea was that human beings – regardless of their social status or accident of birth – are of equal intrinsic worth and deserve the same rights and considerations. Ours was the first civilization to believe in this revolutionary notion. The idea grew haltingly at first, and it took centuries to implement it fully. But eventually the West managed – after a long struggle – to devise a system of institutions and laws that translated this ideal into practical reality. For the West's humanness and boldness to acknowledge the dignity of the ordinary man, "ordinary" men enriched our civilization beyond measure. As the domain of personal autonomy and freedom gradually expanded, gifted individuals could increasingly realize their inborn talents. Their subsequent accomplishments advanced the cause of mankind in nearly every sphere of human existence. Leonardo da Vinci, Michael Faraday, Francisco Goya, Immanuel Kant, Johann Sebastian Bach, Rembrandt, Ludwig van Beethoven as well as many other outstanding human beings were not born into high status or great privilege. Had they been born into a different civilizational stream, it is quite likely most of them would not have had the necessary space and freedom to develop their talents in the way they did. And the world would be much poorer for it.

One of the great steps forward in man's march toward freedom was taken by the bearers of the Western Tradition who sailed from Europe to the New World. There, after breaking away from their transatlantic overlords, American colonists for the first time in history set out to build a society that was consciously based on the recognition that all men are created equal. It took nearly two hundred years to translate this ideal fully into reality, but it was accomplished at last. Because of its willingness to self-correct and pay whatever price it took to set things right, America blossomed in the second half of the 20th century into the freest, most prosperous and technologically advanced society in history. It also led the world in the struggle against the forces of totalitarian darkness which sought to sacrifice the autonomy of the individual on the altar of collectivist utopia.

Prague's Old Town Hall and the Astronomical Clock, America's Declaration of Independence and its Constitution, and a Patek Philippe's *Grandmaster Chime* are some examples of great Western achievements. They are products of a civilization humane enough to acknowledge the dignity of all and wise enough to allow room for inquiry and the questioning of dogma. It is because of these qualities that its outstanding individuals could think of the rights of man, investigate the movement of stars and the flow of time, construct engines and space rockets, and create artifacts of great beauty and sophistication. Ours is not a perfect civilization, but none ever was. Everything considered, however, ours is unquestionably a magnificent one. We should draw upon its centuries of wisdom and be grateful for what our ancestors achieved as they struggled – often in very difficult circumstances – against the limits of nature and the human condition. Their breath-taking achievements are laid out for all of us to see and make use of. The Sistine Chapel, the Rembrandts, the Goyas, the van Goghs, the great astronomical clocks on the walls of old European townhalls, the plays of Shakespeare, the magnificent cathedrals and so much more can all be enjoyed and admired at little or no cost. And even though most of us may not be able to afford a Patek Philippe, just contemplating its sheer elegance and finesse is a reward enough in itself. Knowing that somewhere in a Swiss valley there quietly work master watchmakers who possess the skill and taste to create objects of this kind cannot but fill one's heart with satisfaction and pride in the Tradition that has made this possible.

If you walk from Prague's Old Town Square eastward down a street called Celetná and then make a sharp right turn, you will soon happen upon the Estates Theatre. Built in the late part of the 18th century, it is widely considered to be one of the most beautiful historical theatre buildings in Europe. But apart from being a jewel of neo-classical architecture, the theater also has the distinction of hosting one of the great cultural events in history. On a late autumn day, October 29, 1787, a thirty-one-year-old Wolfgang Amadeus Mozart made his way into the building to conduct the premiere of his newly completed operatic score which he called Don Giovanni. It was here 233 years ago that the world first heard his haunting masterpiece, one of the high points of humanity's cultural history. The sounds teased out by Mozart's baton from the symphony orchestra – which is another great western invention – kept the audience spellbound throughout. The premiere turned out to be a great success. Observed one music critic: "Connoisseurs and musicians say that Prague has never heard the like." And how could they? Mozart's Don Giovanni is unlike any other piece of music ever written. From the overture's thundering D minor cadence through the great Leporello aria to the chilling finale, this operatic masterpiece is a supreme achievement of human creativity. Like the medieval builders of the Old Town Hall Tower, the vivacious Austrian, too, created his time-transcending marvel in the face of mortality and limitation. Barely four years after that triumphant Prague premiere, the broken body of that stupendous genius was buried anonymously in a common grave on the outskirts of Vienna. He was just thirty-five years old.

The Old Town Square, the Great Astronomical Clock, the Patek Phillipe display and the Estates Theater are all in their own way symbolic of that human progress led by the West for the better part of the last thousand years. Within a short walking distance of one another, these are just four of a number of priceless treasures that can be found within less than two square miles of this beautiful European city. We could go on and speak of its other jewels such the Charles Bridge, the Prague Castle, St. Vitus Cathedral, the Powder Gate, Malá Strana and the Golden Lane. Each of them has its own fascinating story engendered by the vibrancy of the great civilization which gave them birth. Perhaps we will speak of them one day too, but what has been said so far is sufficient for what we are trying to put across.

Walking among these marvels one cannot but feel immense love, gratitude and appreciation for the civilization that enabled flawed human beings to create these works of such splendor and beauty. At the same time, there is a creeping feeling of nostalgia. One fears we may be living in the twilight of the Great Western Tradition. In the United States and across Europe its values and spirit have come under an attack it may not be able withstand, mainly due to the listlessness and apathy of its heirs. But whatever the future may hold, those who still care should try their best to stand for what is right, good and precious, because to allow it to be slandered, pulled down and burnt would be catastrophic for the spirit and memory of humanity.

THE REAL TARGET OF 'ANTI-RACISM' PROTESTS: WESTERN CIVILIZATION AND ITS VALUES

I am among those who believe that our Western civilization is on its way to perishing. It has many commendable qualities, most of which it has borrowed from the Christian ethic, but it lacks the element of moral wisdom that would give it permanence. Future historians will record that we of the twentieth century had intelligence enough to create a great civilization but not the moral wisdom to preserve it.
— Aiden Wilson Tozer

T hat Western civilization is in crisis has been obvious to some people for some time. The dramatic events of recent months in America and Europe have brought home with great vividness and immediacy the seriousness of this crisis. The protests and looting that swept through the United States quickly turned dozens of inner American cities into something akin to bombed- out war zones. The surging wave of violence and anarchy, however, was not the only issue of deep concern. Equally alarming was our society's response to it. Instead of taking measures to re-establish order and the rule of law, our political system malfunctioned at the moment of emergency. Fractious and paralyzed, the political establishment not only failed to implement meaningful measures to take control of the situation, it – unbelievably – tied the hands of the law enforcement, forcing it to stand by as destruction unfolded right before our eyes. Rather than encouraging and empowering the police to fight the unfolding anarchy, the events took a truly bizarre twist when some politicians and public officials began cutting funding for the very bodies and agencies tasked with protection of public order.

It is no exaggeration to say that the protests shook our society to its very foundations. They exposed a number of latent fault lines and further exacerbated those that had been painfully obvious before. The situation suddenly appeared to be so dire that many people began to fear that our nation – and indeed the whole of Western society – may be on the brink of disintegration. These fears may well be justified, since America was not the only country so shaken. Protests of similar nature gripped other Western democracies as well.

Most would now agree that the West is in the throes of an existential crisis. What is not so clear or agreed upon, however, is the nature of the crisis or even what the core issues and problems are. This lack of clarity is disconcerting, because if we cannot accurately identify the cause, we cannot take effective measures to address it. The first step toward understanding the nature of our plight, therefore, is to grasp what these protests were really about, since they obviously represented a violent eruption of the discontent and pathologies that have been festering in the Western psyche and which now threaten to engulf and destroy our societies.

The stated reason for these protests – both in the United States and Europe – was racism, which is said to be the great moral failing of our civilization. In the United States especially, we saw protesters asserting with great vehemence and anger that our society is oppressive toward minorities, particularly black people. But for anyone who knows the situation in the United States there was something fundamentally problematic with these assertions: they are false.

Even though it is true that the United States has had a history of racial injustice – as, in fact, almost all countries have – it is definitely not the case today. In a sincere effort to correct past wrongs, in the last sixty years the United States has undertaken tremendous efforts to assist and uplift its black population. This massive multipronged undertaking has been carried out with great resolution and at tremendous cost. It took the form of financial and material assistance, of various types of reverse discrimination, racial quotas in employment and education, preferential treatment of various kinds, lowering of professional and educational standards for black people and a host of other measures. Most of this was motivated by a genuine desire to improve the lives and situation of African Americans.

After six decades of this we can say with complete confidence that never in history has a power-yielding majority done so much for a racial minority as white Americans have done for black Americans. As the writer Fred Reed put it: "In truth, America has made the greatest effort ever essayed by one race to uplift another."[21]

The fact is that not only black people have equal rights – individual, civil, legal and political – with whites, but our current societal system is actually biased in favor of racial minorities. If truth be told, blacks in America today enjoy more protections, rights and advantage than white people do. American whites are the only ruling majority that has voluntarily relinquished its hold on power and made blacks the most protected, financially supported and privileged racial minority in history. This much is obvious to any objective observer.

The claim that the United States is a racist society is thus completely at variance with reality. It is simply not true. One of the countless examples one could mention to illustrate this is the spectacular rise of Barack Obama, who was elected to the highest office in America even though his prior accomplishments would – in the words of one commentator – barely fill the back of a postage stamp. A community organizer with a past of which he did not wish to speak, Mr. Obama's main qualification for becoming President of the United States was apparently the fact that his skin was black. Needless to say, the bulk of the votes that catapulted Mr. Obama into office was cast by white people. Could anything like this ever happen in a racist country?

There are, of course, instances of racism on individual and private levels. All racial groups are prone to this kind of prejudice and black people are no exception. In fact, black racism is a well-known phenomenon, and it is probably more widespread and corrosive than white on black racism today. But be that as it may, any public manifestation of vestigial private racism against minorities – whether it be in employment, education, politics or in any other area – is quickly dealt with by a range of mechanisms designed to stop and correct any such occurrences. Acts of racism or discrimination are unlawful in the United States and the country enforces its anti-discriminatory laws with considerable vigor and strictness. So much so that the law is often abused in the opposite direction. Few countries are more sensitive to the issue of racism than the US. Rather than being discriminatory, American society as it exists now is structured in a way to give minorities advantage over the majority.

This is not to deny that large parts of the black community are plagued by severe pathologies and ills. But these are not the result of discrimination. The seventy- five percent illegitimacy rate and the decadent black street culture are among some of the root causes of the black predicament. The chances of a child born to a single mother who grows up in the grip of black street culture – as so many black children do – to become an upright, well-adjusted human being who can lead a fulfilling life are virtually zero. This, we would suggest, is the real driver of the black crisis. In other words, the problems that plague the black demographic are moral in nature and not a consequence of racism.

To give legitimacy to their claims, race activists point to instances like the George Floyd incident. But in a nation of more than 320 million people in which every year there are more than three million police-public contacts such events are extremely rare. Studies and investigations have repeatedly shown that the police do not apply lethal force in a racially biased manner. In the vast majority of cases where black men die in the hands of the police, it is not because they are targeted for the color of their skin. This may also have been the case with George Floyd as there is a substantial body of evidence that his death was a result of cardiopulmonary arrest brought about by a combination of pre-existing conditions with lethal levels of Fentanyl in his system.[22]

But even if George Floyd was killed by a rogue cop because of the color of his skin, it would not indicate that America as such is a racist nation. There are bad cops, of course, as there are bad, lawyers, doctors and teachers. That, however, does not mean that such individuals are reflective of the society as a whole. Such bad apples are exceptions and whenever their actions are brought to light they are dealt with by appropriate mechanisms. This is most certainly the case with the police where every lethal event is subject to extensive inquiry and investigation.

Protests in Britain

The false basis of the protests that swept across large portions of the western world become even more obvious when we look at the situation on the other side of the Atlantic. Not long after rioting broke out in the US, similar events began to occur in Great Britain as well. As in the US, the protests there were organized by Black Lives Matter and featured almost identical rhetoric and posturing. Like in the United States, the declared cause of the protests was racism which is – so it was alleged – endemically and systemically embedded in British society.

There was, however, a jarring incoherence in the whole enterprise. Even though the protests were ostensibly about the supposedly pervasive racism in Britain, they were launched and conducted in the name of George Floyd. The question that arises is this: If you are protesting racism in the UK, why do you do it in the name of a man who had nothing to do with the UK? George

Floyd was not a British citizen, had no ties to Britain and died thousands of miles away in another country. His death had absolutely nothing to do with British society, the British government or the British police. Why, then, do the protesters who demonstrate against the alleged racial injustices in the UK carry posters of George Floyd and chant his name as they march along? If they are protesting racism in the UK, why don't they bring up instances of racism from Great Britain? If Britain is such a racist country as they say it is, they should have no difficulties pointing to genuine home-made instances of racial oppression. Why don't they do it then?

The answer is quite simple: It is because they cannot not really find any. Rather than being oppressed, the black minority in the UK enjoys similar kinds of special protections, privileges, rights and benefits that are enjoyed by their counterparts across the ocean. The UK, like America, is not racist country... far from it. Like the United States, the UK has bent backwards to help and accommodate its racial minorities whom it treats with great consideration and good will. Hence the difficulties of the protestors to find an authentic homemade cause around which to rally their movement. Instead, they had to disingenuously exploit an unfortunate and unrepresentative incident that happened an ocean away in a country not their own.

What all this shows is that the "anti-racism" protests that took place on both sides of the Atlantic were launched and conducted on a fraudulent basis and under false pretenses. The protestors were thus literally rebels without a cause. Or, to be more precise, they were rebels with a fake cause. Their fake cause was systemic racism which, however, they could not document with any bona fide evidence.

The movement's true objective

The question, then, becomes: What was the real reason for the protests? What were these protests in their core really about?

Before we go further, we should observe that the protestors

did not form a monolithic front. They were made of various groups, subgroups and factions who took part for various reasons and with different agendas. They ranged from looters who come to get their free Nike shoes and iPhones through spoilt white college students in search of meaning to aging boomers who longed to relive the excitement of their 60s heyday. There were also those who were seeking an outlet for the surfeit of their energies generated by the prolonged COVID lockdowns, and then there were the menacing Antifa types.

Yet despite all of this variance of groups and motives, the overall thrust and energy inclined in a specific direction and against a definite target. We can see what that target was when we consider the kind of symbolic objects the protestors targeted for physical destruction. One class of such objects were the statues representing distinguished men of the past. Revealingly, the mob was not after a particular group of historical figures. The statue slayers attacked memorials of men who distinguished themselves across the spectrum of human endeavors – thinkers, national leaders, explorers, religious figures. Even though the destruction was carried out under the generic charge of racism, many people were startled by its apparently indiscriminate and random nature. The attacks, however, were not random in the deeper sense, for what these men shared was that they all played some part in the advancement and progress of Western civilization. In other words, each in his own way contributed in some measure to the flourishing of Western culture. And it was precisely this fact that drew the ire of the raging mob. The racism charge with which they sought to cover their motives was purely nominal and obviously false, given that they targeted statues even of men who had done much in the cause of liberation of black people. Abraham Lincoln would be one example of this.

But even the attacks on men who have done less for minorities than Lincoln did were contrary to reason, since their contributions helped to build the only civilization in human history that grants racial minorities equal freedoms and rights. If the protestors were indeed concerned with racial progress, they would feel gratitude toward these individuals. Their attacks, however, reveal what these protests were actually about – an attack on Western civilization and culture.

But it is not only the crass destruction of physical symbols that betray the protestors' true motivation. Underneath these crude physical gestures is a more subtle and far more dangerous assault on the foundational values and principles of Western culture such as freedom of speech, open discourse, freedom of expression, tolerance of opposing views and freedom of conscience. This we will discuss in in the pages that follow.

For now, we leave you with this observation: It is hatred of the West that is the true driver of the faux "anti-racist" crusade. It is this, rather than the non-existent racism, that represents an existential threat to our societies and way of life.

THE MYTH OF SYSTEMIC RACISM: IN AMERICA REVERSE DISCRIMINATION IS THE NORM

E arlier we have attempted to bring to light the real motives behind the "anti-racism" crusade that has been sweeping through the Western world. We have argued that its objective is not to correct racial injustice but to subvert Western societies. The inability of social justice warriors to give genuine examples of societally sanctioned racism shows the true nature of this movement.

The most frequently used argument in support of the claim of systemic racism is the use of force by police against blacks, which it is claimed, is disproportional and racially motivated. This, it is said, is symptomatic of the intrinsically racist nature of American society which uses law enforcement to harass and oppress minorities.

There is a scenario that regularly takes place in connection with this narrative. An African American is shot by the police. Before there is time to hear the full story of what happened, the news quickly spreads that the police have "murdered" or "executed" an innocent black person. The man in question is usually described as a peaceful individual who was just going about his business. Upon hearing this, cries of injustice are heard and protests break out. Jesse Jackson, Al Sharpton and other activists arrive to give speeches. When the facts of the case finally emerge in full, however, it usually turns out that the suspect was actually a violent person with a long criminal record and the incident in question took place while he posed deadly danger to those around him.

This is not to say that policemen do not make mistakes, harm innocent people or employ excessive force on some occasions. This does happen and such offences need to be dealt with. Almost everyone agrees that cops who deliberately misuse their power should be prosecuted and punished. There is, however, no evidence that there exists a systemic pattern of abuse along racial lines. And study after study has demonstrated this. A recent article in the Wall Street Journal titled "The Myth of Systemic Police Racism" states: "A solid body of evidence finds no structural bias in the criminal-justice system with regard to arrests, prosecution or sentencing. Crime and suspect behavior, not race, determine most police actions."

The article, then, goes on to give actual data and facts:

> In 2019 police officers fatally shot 1,004 people, most of whom were armed or otherwise dangerous. African Americans were about a quarter of those killed by cops last year (235), a ratio that has remained stable since 2015. That share of black victims is less than what the black crime rate would predict, since police shootings are a function of how often officers encounter armed and violent suspects. In 2018, the latest year for which such data have been published, African Americans made up 53% of known homicide offenders in the U.S. and commit about 60% of robberies, though they are 13% of the population.[23]

Notice this: fewer blacks die at the hands of police than would be expected given the crime ratios. Even though more than half of violent criminals are black, they constitute about one quarter of suspects shot by law enforcement. In other words, black criminals are disproportionally less likely to be killed than white criminals.

Exactly the same conclusion was arrived at by Roland Fryer who is a professor of Economics at Harvard University. Professor Fryer also happens to be black. A few years ago, he conducted an extensive study in which he investigated how the use of police force plays out among various racial groups. This is how the results of the study have been reported just after it came out: "There is no racial bias when officers fire on suspects, according to a new study by Prof. Roland Fryer – black suspects are actually less likely to be shot than other suspects."[24] To put it in different words, studies keep demonstrating that there seems to be reverse discrimination when it comes to the use of lethal force against crime suspects.

Fryer called his findings "the most surprising result" of his career. He speculated that the comparative leniency toward black criminals was due to the disproportionate legal and psychological costs that are incurred by officers as a result of fatal events involving African Americans. His reasoning is probably correct, for we rarely see special prosecutions, protests and burning cities after white suspects are shot by the police.

This documented leniency, however, does not earn officers much good will from the lawbreaking community. As the Wall Street Journal points out: "A police officer is 18½ times more likely to be killed by a black male than an unarmed black male is to be killed by a police officer." So much for the charge of "black genocide" which is casually thrown around by champions of social justice.

Apart from the demonstrably false charge of police racism, social justice warriors do not really offer any other believable examples in support of their claims. Even while they make their sweeping accusations of structural, institutional and systemic racism, they actually offer no credible evidence to back up their assertions. Revealingly, this deficiency plagues the anti-racism movement on both sides of the Atlantic. A couple of months ago there was an eye-opening interview with an activist who participated in the protests that were at the time convulsing Britain. In the course of the interview, he was asked whether he could give specific examples of racism in the UK. Instead of citing some concrete instances, the activist replied that specifics do not matter. What really matters, he declared, is the overall atmosphere.

This should make everyone pause and think. If the US and the UK were indeed racist societies, the protestors should have no difficulties citing numerous real-life instances of racism. But this they almost never do. What they do instead is to level sweeping but nebulous condemnations. Specifics, of course, matter. They, in fact, matter supremely, for if our societies suffer from pervasive racism then that would be the result of specific, identifiable practices, actions, laws and rules. If we want to end racial discrimination, we have to begin with something concrete. What measures can be taken or what laws can be passed on the basis of the vague and unspecific assertions of systemic racism? What do phrases such as "systemic" "structural" or "institutional" racism even mean in absence of any specifics? The protestors need to show where the alleged racism actually resides and what forms it takes. Otherwise, it is impossible to do anything about it.

In the Jim Crow era – when there was real racism in this country – the activists of that time could easily point to specific laws and practices that were racist. It was easy to see where racism was and how it was maintained and perpetuated. People of good will had something to work with and subsequently progress could be made, i.e., it was obvious which discriminatory laws needed to be repealed and what practices had to be eliminated in order to achieve racial justice.

Today, however, no discriminatory laws or practices are cited by the protestors. Lacking in specificity, therefore, their allegations of systemic racism are empty and thus unactionable. Rather than to rectify genuine injustices, the main objective behind such claims seems to be the desire to evoke guilt for the purpose of obtaining political power. Shelby Steele's observation, which he made more than a decade ago, seems to apply perfectly today:

> [I] know it [white guilt] to be something very specific: the vacuum of moral authority that comes from simply knowing that one's race is associated with racism. Whites (and American institutions) must acknowledge historical racism to show themselves redeemed of it, but once they acknowledge it they lose moral authority over everything having to do with race, equality, social justice, poverty, and so on. They step into a void of vulnerability. The authority they lose transfers to the 'victims' of historical racism and becomes their great power in society. This is why white guilt is quite literally the same thing as black power.[25]

Shelby Steele should know about these matters, since he is speaking from personal experience. If you did not know, Steele is black and he himself was part of a group that used such tactics with good effect during his student days.

We would suggest that there is a good reason for why social warriors of today do not present any genuine evidence for their claims: There is none. American society, as well as other western democracies, are no racist regimes and as such they have no institutionalized racist practices and laws. And even though this observation may startle those who have succumbed to the prevailing official narrative – which is that we are all racists – it is true nevertheless. Not only is today's narrative false, but the opposite is actually the case: Our system is strongly biased in favor of the black minority. In other words, we discriminate against the majority – and certain high-achieving minorities – for the purpose advantaging selected minorities, especially African Americans. Rather than practicing systemic racism our society in reality practices systemic *reverse* racism.

Unlike the social warriors who complain of systemic racism, the fact of systemic *reverse* racism can be documented with hundreds of real-life examples. Only last week, for example, the US Department of Justice found that Yale University discriminated against white and Asian students. According to a piece in the Wall Street Journal, the Department concluded after its investigation that

> Yale discriminates based on race and national origin, violating federal civil-rights law, and that race was the 'determinative factor' in hundreds of admissions decisions each year. It said for the majority of applicants, Asian-American and white students have one-tenth to one-fourth the likelihood of being admitted as African American applicants with comparable academic credentials.[26]

Commenting on the finding, Pat Buchanan points out: "If the definition of racism is deliberate discrimination based on race, color or national origin, Yale University appears to be a textbook case of 'systemic racism.'" Yale will undoubtedly receive a great deal of criticism for this, but the practice for which this university has been singled out is actually widespread among institutions of higher learning across the United States.

Harvard, for example, has also been in hot water for the same issue. The case against Harvard was brought on by Asian applicants who filed a lawsuit on the grounds of discrimination.[27] In the process, the plaintiffs compelled the university to disclose some of its admission procedures, and it turns out – from the information available so far – that Harvard engages in a kind of racial profiling one would not think possible in 21st century America. During the application process, the university apparently assigns points for applicants' race, and if you happen to be an Asian American you suffer a deduction in the "personal rating" column. The net result is that many highly accomplished Asian Americans are excluded in favor of black candidates who are far less qualified. Even though in an earlier ruling the presiding judge acknowledged Harvard's discrimination, he used rather tortuous reasoning to try to justify this behavior. The case is now headed for the Supreme Court and many observers think it will not go well for Harvard given all the facts that have come to light. The Ivy Leagues, however, are not the only institutions that struggle with this issue. We could go right down the list and name a hundred other US schools that engage in the same or worse practices.

But there is an even deeper point to be made. The reverse-discrimination that exists in higher education is emblematic of our society as a whole. The truth is that American society practices this kind of racism in almost every sphere of life: education, employment, government contracting, cash transfers, social support, etc. Most of these programs are calibrated – in subtle and not so subtle ways – in a manner that favors minorities in general and African Americans in particular.

Here is the crux of the matter: Social justice activists claim that America is a racist society that systemically discriminates against black people, but they fail to submit any genuine evidence in support their claims. In the absence of such evidence, it has to be concluded that their allegations are not true. On the other hand, it is quite obvious that there exists reverse discrimination all throughout our society that favors black Americans. This observation can be easily backed up with hundreds of genuine real-life, documentable examples of social and institutional practice.

Facts ultimately decide the truth of any issue, not unsupported assertions. Protesting, screaming and cancelling opposing views does not make activists' attestations any truer. In fact, such behavior only puts into sharper relief the hollowness of their claims.

Our appeal is this: let us not tear down this society under false pretenses. Let us look at our situation soberly and fix whatever needs fixing. We are not perfect and there are many issues that need to be addressed. Our society, for example, suffers from a serious moral decline which has affected all demographics across the spectrum, but has hit the black community especially hard. Most black children grow up without their fathers under the influence of noxious street culture, which is a combination that effectively destroys their prospects of good life. Let us encourage and support black men to be present as fathers and provide good examples to their children. Let us encourage ourselves to be such as well, because God knows that we all need help in these challenging times. Another area of deep concern is chronic debt throughout all strata of our society which threatens to devalue our currency and cause an economic collapse the likes of which America has never seen before.

These are some of the problems that urgently need to be tackled now if we want to survive as a functioning country. Although the United States has had a history of racial discrimination, racism is not a problem in America at this time. And if anyone feels that it is a problem, let them be constructive and show us where exactly it resides so that we can take care of it.

Loathing the West: The Real Reason Why "Anti-Racism" Protestors Desecrate Christian Churches

Though this be madness, yet there is method in't.
— William Shakespeare, Hamlet (Act II, Scene II)

"Last weekend, at least four Catholic Church-affiliated buildings and statues from Boston to Los Angeles were set on fire or vandalized. A blaze that gutted the 249-year-old San Gabriel Mission, once led by Father Junipero Serra, is being investigated as possible arson" reported the Washington Times on July 15. The piece was titled "'No place for God': Left-Wing Protesters Turn Focus to Churches As Vandalism, Arson Escalate."

The article quoted Catholic Action League Executive Director C. J. Doyle who said: "Given that there were four attacks on Catholic churches nationwide over a 48-hour period, from July 10 to July 12, suspicion, obviously, turns toward the leftwing extremists who have been toppling statues of Saint Junipero Serra and attempting to remove a statue of Saint Louis."

On June 1, the Catholic News Agency put out a wire headlined "Churches in 6 States Damaged by Violent Protests." It read in part:

> Church buildings in California, Minnesota, New York, Kentucky, Texas, and Colorado were attacked. Many of the defaced or damaged churches were cathedrals. The Cathedral Basilica of the Immaculate Conception in Denver sustained permanent damage. Vandals repeatedly struck the Denver cathedral on multiple nights of the protests and riots over the weekend. The church building and rectory were spray painted with the slogans "Pedofiles" [sic], "God is dead," "There is no God," along with other anti-police, anarchist, and anti-religion phrases and symbols.[28]

On July 22, the Wall Street Journal published a piece called "Desecration of Catholic Churches Across U.S. Leaves Congregations Shaken." The sub-headline was: "More than half a dozen incidents in recent weeks include arson, decapitation of statues of Jesus and the Virgin Mary." The piece opened as follows:

> Parishioners and clergy were shocked and grieving following a spate of vandalism at Catholic churches in various U.S. cities in recent weeks. Catholic institutions from Boston to Florida reported more than half a dozen attacks on church property, including statues of Jesus and the Virgin Mary, between July 10 and 16.[29]

On July 21, the CNS network released an item headlined "Statue of Jesus beheaded in Florida among latest attacks on Catholic churches." It began:

> The beheading of a statue of Christ at a Catholic church in the Miami Archdiocese has saddened the parish community of Good Shepherd Church and prompted Miami Archbishop Thomas G. Wenski to call on law enforcement to investigate the incident as a hate crime. On July 15, the statue at Good Shepherd Catholic Church in Southwest Miami-Dade was found with its head chopped off and knocked from its pedestal.[30]

"Churches burned and vandalized in riots"[31] announced a headline from the Washington Examiner. The article commenced with this sentence: "Several churches were burned and vandalized over the weekend as protests of police brutality turned to rioting and looting in many American cities." Three paragraphs later we learned that "St. Patrick's Cathedral in New York City, one of the most famous churches in America, was vandalized Saturday night with references to the Black Lives Matter movement and the F-word."

The question that arises is this: Why would those marching under the auspices of Black Lives Matter while protesting the death of George Floyd attack Christian churches? What exactly is the logical link between their professed cause – which is anti-racism – and their onslaught on Christian houses of worship?

Christianity, after all, played no part in the unfortunate George Floyd incident. There is no indication that the officers involved in his arrest were motivated by religious sentiments. In the days that followed, Christian pastors and figures across the spectrum unanimously expressed grief over Floyd's death and churches across the land conducted services and held vigils in his name.

The violence of "anti-racism" protestors against Christian symbols and houses of worship has left many people startled and confused. Understandably so, since there seems to be no detectable link between the demonstrators stated goals and their actions. This obvious contradiction was pointed out by Valerie Richardson writing in the Washington Times: "It would be quite a stretch to blame churches for George Floyd's death, police brutality or Confederate memorials, yet houses of worship and religious statues are coming under attack in the protest mayhem."[32]

To say it would be "quite a stretch" is an understatement. The protestors' rhetoric and behavior would appear outright self-contradictory, and yet one cannot but feel that there is a method in this apparent madness. Why, then, we ask, do champions of racial justice attack sacred Christian objects? Why do they behead statues of Jesus and topple those of the Virgin Mary?

Their behavior will appear inexplicable only as long as we accept at face value the stated goal of the protests, which, they say, is the elimination of racism. Racial justice, however, is *not* what this movement is about. We have already stated that the actual purpose of this "anti-racism" campaign is the vitiation of Western civilization. Once we clearly grasp this truth, the apparently irrational blitz on Christian artifacts will no longer seem incoherent. It will, in fact, make perfect sense.

Along with our Greco-Roman heritage, Christianity has been one of the two great pillars of Western culture. It was Catholic Christianity that kept the light of civilization through the Dark Ages in Europe and that subsequently carried the continent into the Renaissance and beyond. It was Catholic Christianity that inspired and brought into being the magnificent Cathedrals of Europe and the sublime marbles of Michelangelo and all of the great art in between. It was the great theologians of the Church who spoke of the infinite worth of the human soul and prepared that ground for the revolutionary idea that all human beings – no matter how great or small – are entitled to equal considerations and rights. (Tellingly, the West is not the only civilization that believes this, but it is the only one that has implemented this idea in practice.) Later it was the Protestant ethic of hard work, frugality and deferred gratification that helped fuel the forces of free market capitalism which generated unprecedented levels of prosperity for ordinary people. We could speak for hours about the countless ways in which Christianity – both of the Catholic and Protestant kind – shaped and advanced Western civilization. But this is not necessary, since its influence is obvious. Much of our culture, our moral sensibility, our ethical codes, the manner in which we conduct our societal life and, in fact, the very way we look at the world derive directly or indirectly from the Christian religion.

Therefore, any movement seeking to undermine Western civilization must sooner or later turn on the West's Christian heritage. This is inevitable. Being such a movement, the "anti-racism" crusade that is sweeping across Western democracies has done exactly that. The moment we grasp the fact that this movement is fueled and driven by Atropic hatred, the attacks of these so-called anti-racist protestors on Christian symbols seem completely natural and predictable.

We spoke previously about how the protestors' attacks on the statues of great men who contributed to the advancement of the West is driven by their anti-Western agenda. The desecration of Christian churches is born of the same psychological impulse – aversion toward Western civilization and the desire to bring it down.

There are many aspects of the protestors' behavior that reveal what they are truly about. For example, if they were genuinely concerned about racism, they would surely stage at least some of their events in front of mosques. Mosques, as most people know, represent a civilizational stream that has been pronouncedly racist. Not only do most Islamic societies engage in blatant racist practices to this very day, they actually see nothing wrong with it. And yet the self-proclaimed anti-racism protestors voice no complaints in that direction. Do you see the contradiction here?

It is worrisome that so many people do not see through this. This fact is attested by the vast amounts of donations from individuals, organizations and corporations to various social justice groups and especially Black Lives Matter, the organization under whose auspices these faux protests are conducted. *The New York Times* ran a piece in June titled "Racial Justice Groups Flooded With Millions in Donations"[33] in which it reported that such groups received 90 million dollars in contributions for their bail funds alone. The bail funds are, of course, used to assist those arrested for the widespread violence and criminal destruction of public and private property that has been taking place during these "protests."

There are, however, some people who see the truth of the matter. One of them is Ken Blackwell, a former U.S. ambassador to the U.N. Human Rights Commission. This is what he said: "These folks have an agenda, which is to fundamentally transform America."[34] Ken Blackwell is correct. The vandals' objective is not, as so many people assume, to eliminate injustice from our society. Since, as we have pointed out, in the United States and in other Western democracies institutional racism does not exist, objections against it cannot be genuine. The intention is not to fix a racial problem, but to tear down those societies against which false charge have been levelled. The attack on Christianity is part and parcel of this undertaking.

This project is not confined to the United States. Most Americans do not realize there have been many attacks on Christian sites in Europe. According to a report from Gatestone Institute:

[R]oughly 3,000 Christian churches, schools, cemeteries

and monuments were vandalized, looted or defaced in Europe during 2019 — which is on track to becoming a record year for anti-Christian sacrilege on the continent. Violence against Christian sites is most widespread in France, where churches, schools, cemeteries and monuments are being vandalized, desecrated and burned at an average rate of three per day, according to government statistics. In Germany, attacks against Christian churches are occurring at an average rate of two per day, according to police blotters. Attacks on Christian churches and symbols are also commonplace in Belgium, Britain, Denmark, Ireland, Italy and Spain. The attacks overwhelmingly involve Roman Catholic sites and symbols, although in Germany, Protestant churches are also being targeted.[35]

As Atropos waxes, it can only be expected that such attacks will further accelerate both in Europe and the US. The protestors themselves make their intentions quite clear, barely attempting to conceal their true motives. In many cases they do not bother to make even tenuous links between their bogus cause of "anti-racism" and their attacks on Christianity. In fact, they are surprisingly brazen about their goals. By inscribing slogans such as "God is dead," and "There is no God" and by drawing anarchist and pagan graffiti on the walls of Christian edifices, these self-styled protestors could not be clearer about what they really want.

Just think about it: What do pagan symbols have to do with the struggle for racial justice? Have pagan cultures ever been known for their racial tolerance or equality? Have they ever been known to treat minorities with compassion and understanding? Anyone who knows anything about history knows that there has been little social justice in pagan cultures. As a rule, the way pagan societies treat their minorities is appalling. To express this truth in modern idiom, pagan cultures almost invariably discriminate – often brutally – on the basis of race, gender, national original, disability, sexual orientation and on the basis of whatever else that can make one different from the ruling elite in charge. The only societies that have treated minorities with understanding and compassion have been those arising from the Western civilizational stream. Western societies are the only ones in history in which minorities are given the full measure of human respect and equal rights. As far as we know, there have been no significant social justice movements in pagan societies. This should not surprise, since any would-be activists against oppression in non-Christian cultures usually come to a quick end.

Pagan cultures do not suffer social warriors gladly. The only truly successful social justice movement in the world – one that has fought for equal rights for all people – has been the civilizing influence of the Christian culture. It is only after non-western societies come into contact with the West that their minorities can hope for fair treatment and equal rights. Why, then, today's Western "anti-racist" warriors defile Christian churches with pagan symbols and crass obscenities? The anarchist signs – painted right next to the pagan ones – tell us what they are really after: the toppling of our society.

The evidence the protestors leave behind unmistakably shows that their desecration of Christian artifacts has nothing to do with concerns about racism. Rather it is an expression of an aversion toward Western civilization of which Christianity has been a great pillar. The incoherent rhetoric and self-contradictory behavior make it plain that it is the subversion of Western culture that is the ultimate goal of today's "social justice" movement.

THE AIM OF SOCIAL JUSTICE MOVEMENT IS SUBVERSION OF CORE WESTERN VALUES

I wrote earlier about what the attacks on statues and churches that have been taking place as part of the BLM protests reveal about the nature of this movement. They show that these protests are not actuated by a desire to bring about racial justice, but by hatred of Western culture. It is *not* the elimination of non-existent racism that is the objective of this crusade. Its real goal is the destruction of liberal democracy.

Beneath the crass attacks on the physical artifacts of Western tradition, however, a less obvious but far more destructive assault is being launched: it is an assault on the core values and principles of Western civilization. It is an onslaught on the very values that have made its accomplishments possible. The Western miracle came about because certain ideas gained hold in the occidental psyche, and it was these principles that enabled the Western mind to create a civilization that has advanced, flourished and excelled in ways unmatched by any other.

One of the quintessential, and arguably the most important, among these values is freedom of expression. The Western achievement could not have taken place without it. Conversely, it is the lack of this freedom that is the main reason why other civilizations lag behind in almost every metric. It is not difficult to see why, since it is through an open exchange of ideas and sympathetic consideration of differing points of view that true learning and progress take place. Similarly, by giving room to creative individuals to express the innermost stirrings of their souls, great works of art and spirit are created.

It is freedom of expression that lies behind the West's spectacular attainments in the arts, architecture, literature, science, music, technology and nearly every other area of human endeavor. Freedom of expression – particularly in its manifestation as free speech – is the essential prerequisite for one of the West's crowning achievements: liberal democracy. Western democracy, as some may know, is the *only* form of societal organization that grants and guarantees equal rights to all people living within it. It is also the only form of government capable of generating freedom and prosperity for the common man. Needless to say, like the marbles of Michelangelo, the symphonies of Beethoven or the paintings of Rembrandt, liberal democracy is a singularly Western achievement.

Freedom of expression has had a long tradition in Western culture. It can be traced more than 2,500 years back to ancient Greece. It is clearly seen at work, for example, in the great dialogues of Plato where participants openly and freely exchange their views and ideas. And even though the scope of permissiveness of the freedom of expression has fluctuated through the centuries, it has always run like a continuous thread through the current of western history. We can get a sense of the value of this freedom and the kind of wide-ranging beneficial dialogue it engenders from an observation made by the late Sir Roger Scruton:

> All of the great scientists of our time, when you look back at Einstein and Freud and Piaget, and all those people, they were highly cultivated... And for them the intellectual development could have never been con-

fined to something like a laboratory. It was a form of *dialogue* with civilization as a whole.[36]

Given that the current social justice movement is an expression of the Atropic anti-Western animus, it would be expected that those caught up in it would turn against this foundational western value. This they, in fact, do, and they do it with great enthusiasm and fervor. We have seen a startling manifestation of it recently in the rapid rise of the cancel culture which has taken over many of our important public institutions with astonishing speed. And we also see it in the extreme forms of political correctness which is being practiced and advocated by the apostles of social justice.

Political correctness is the instrument of choice for those on the political Left in their drive to do away with freedom of expression. What political correctness does is to prevent the articulation of facts that are plainly obvious but inconvenient to those who seek power by illicit and undemocratic means. As most people have noticed by now, in an environment ruled by political correctness truth must not be spoken. Instead, one must either stay silent or say the *opposite* of the truth. Those who cross the bounds of acceptable discourse are condemned and penalized.

Every oppressive society in history without exception has had its own form of political correctness. In every such society you were not allowed to state the obvious about the nature of that society and the relations within it. If you did, you would be promptly punished. In dictatorial societies political correctness is enforced directly by the state, and it is called censorship.

In the socialist society I grew up in, we had our own strain of strict political correctness. Although its language may have superficially differed from the language of today's western progressives, the principle was exactly the same: we were not allowed to say the truth. In our case the truth was that we were an economically backward country and a vassal of the Soviet Union. The Soviet Union itself was a deeply impoverished nation held together by a brutal police state operating under the banner of a convoluted kind of collectivist ideology which was officially called Marxism-Leninism.

We were, however, not allowed to say what a bad situation this was. Rather we had to say that we lived in a very prosperous and free country and that the Soviet Union was our great benefactor. As for the Soviet Union itself, we had to agree that it was the freest and most affluent country in the world. All people in the Soviet Union were supremely happy because of the abundant prosperity and the freedoms they enjoyed. There was no place on earth or in heaven more excellent than the Soviet Union. Thanks to the great work of Marx, Lenin and Stalin, mankind's long dream of Paradise had at last come true in the great country of the USSR. And guess what was the worst place on earth? It was the United States of America, which was, so were we told, a land of tyranny where people had no real freedoms and where everyone was poor, miserable, oppressed and depressed. As an aside, it is remarkable to observe on how many points the views and rhetoric of the former communists and today's progressives are virtually identical.

The communist politically correct rhetoric ran in complete contravention of reality, but we all had to pretend that it was true. Most people did not believe it, but there were some who did or wanted to. That something like this could take place in real life may seem unbelievable to reasonable people now but lies of similar depth and magnitude are quite commonplace in many Western quarters today.

Consider this politically correct lie: Western societies are oppressive toward women. This is about as absurd a statement as the claim that the Soviet Union was a free country. To everyone with the eyes to see it is quite plain that women are *not* oppressed in Western democracies. On the other hand, women are almost invariably oppressed in non-Western societies. This truth, however, is not allowed to be articulated and most attempts to do so are met with severe consequences, especially for those involved in public institutions such as the media, universities, government and even many corporations.

Here is another politically correct lie: in Western democracies minorities are oppressed. Such assertions are completely false. Rather than being oppressed, racial minorities in the United States and most western countries enjoy more protections and privileges than the majority. This is the reason why minorities from non-western societies are so eager to come and settle in western societies. Conversely, we do not see minorities living in Western democracies running away from their oppression to those supposedly wonderful non-Western societies of which multiculturalists are so fond. Why do you think this is? The reality of the situation and the behavior of people themselves utterly disprove the official PC narrative. Any intimations of the obvious, however, immediately draws the ire of the politically correct organs and can result in prompt cancellation.

The cancel culture is the executory arm of political correctness. Things have become so extreme recently that people are now being cancelled for making even the most innocuous comments. The forms that cancellation can take at this time range from being publicly shamed through removal from platforms of public discourse and having one's reputation destroyed to being dismissed from employment. Given its Atropic nature, it is no surprise today's social justice movement stands as an irreconcilable enemy of free speech. The social warriors' position has its roots in a deep illiberal impulse that goes directly against the best principles of Western culture.

Suppression of free expression has been invariably practiced by totalitarians and tyrants of all ranks and species, whether they emerged from the West or from other civilizational streams. Joseph Stalin, Adolph Hitler, Mao Tse-tung, Pol Pot, Fidel Castro, Kim Jong Un were all sworn enemies of free speech as are present-day anti-racism activists. All these tyrants instituted their own kind of political correctness and cancel culture. Today's social justice warriors are thus firmly rooted in the oppressive tradition of those leaders. The politically correct, cancel-happy progressives who march through the streets of

Western cities and lord it over the social media platforms are the true heirs of these leaders' intolerant, illiberal impulse, which is deeply anti-Western in nature. Needless to say, all the Great Leaders mentioned above have thoroughly ruined their societies and left a trail of misery and corpses in their wake.

Free expression and free speech are, of course, not the only core Western values that have come under attack from the hard left. Others include the concept of private property, the idea of equal rights and equality before the law among others. Like their tyrannical predecessors, the woke progressives of today are not interested in constructively addressing the real problems of their society. Carried along by Atropos' destructive energy, they want to bring down the whole system. Most of them have no clear conception of what should replace it. What they know, however, is that they want nothing to do with the high principles of free speech, truth telling, tolerance of dissent, respect for private property and so on. The main problem with this approach is that societies not based on these values are not good places to live. Just ask the people of Stalin's Soviet Union, Hitler's Nazi Germany, Kim's North Korea, Castro's Cuba or Pol Pot's Cambodia.

WHAT MOTIVATES AMERICA'S REVOLUTIONISTS?

"Revolution is the solution, not voting!"[37] chanted a group of kneeling protestors in Manhattan in June this year.

"Our fight for liberty, justice, and freedom continues. Together, we can — and will — transform. This is the revolution,"[38] reads a posting on the website of Black Lives Matter. In the accompanying video the narrator says, "We continue the tradition of revolution. We feel earth shifting beneath our feet... Now it's time to transform. Together change is coming."

"Milwaukee's Protest Leaders Say 'This Is the Revolution'"[39] proclaims last week's magazine headline.

Another writer observes: "These are not just riots; this is a revolution to change America."[40]

"This Is a Revolution! "declares the title of a piece on the website called "The 74 Million."[41]

In recent months it has become clear that we are in the midst of a revolutionary push whose objective is nothing less than a complete remaking of our society. The assault has been coming not only from the crowds in the streets but also from other corners such as academia, the media, and even the highest reaches of the US government. Recently, for example, Ilhan Omar, a member of the US House of representatives, has openly called for a dismantling of the American way of life as we know it:

> We can't stop at criminal justice reform or policing reform. We are not merely fighting to tear down the systems of oppression in the criminal justice system. We are fighting to tear down systems of oppression that exist in housing, in education, in health care, in employment, [and] in the air we breathe.[42]

Omar's revolutionary zeal has been shared by many of her colleagues in government who have been more discrete than herself, but who have nevertheless done all they can to further the cause. One of the many ways in which they do this is by implementing legislation that ties the hands of law enforcement in order to set loose the insurgent mobs that have been burning our cities and terrorizing America's communities.

In the past five months, the insurrectionists have made impressive gains by changing America's mindset and forcing their agenda on our nation. In this short time, they have been able to dramatically reshape the way many Americans perceive themselves and their country. It is now commonly accepted in many quarters that America is a racist and oppressive nation. America's history has been retold as a tale of oppression and iniquity. Statues of our great men have been desecrated and removed. Scores of Americans are now ashamed of their country, of their past and of themselves as the issue of race has emerged as the foremost consideration in virtually every aspect of our life. The hard-left activists have forced upon many Americans the idea that they are racists. They have convinced us that our racism is subconscious and that any attempt to deny this fact constitutes clear evidence of its existence. To drive their point home, the revolutionists have terrorized our neighborhoods, disrupted our way of life and injured countless people. For good measure they have torched dozens of cities and caused billions of dollars in damage in what the insurance industry has described as "riot and civil disorder"[43] catastrophe in multiple states.

The revolutionaries have been able to achieve all this with astonishing speed and without much resistance. Many people have been puzzled by why there has been so little opposition to this subversive movement, which is based on untruths and furthered by violence. The answer is quite simple: the absence of a pushback is due to the fact that the rioters have been able to seize the high moral ground.

The notion that the revolutionaries are driven by lofty and noble goals has become the unquestioned foundation of the official narrative. It is the desire for justice and equity, we are told, that motivates these people. What they want is to end racism, oppression and discrimination. Having managed to clad themselves in a garb of righteousness, their actions and persons have become almost sacrosanct. Their allegedly noble motives sanctify whatever they say or do, no matter how outrageous or criminal. Because of their allegedly lofty aims, their assertions and demands must not be questioned or their acts second-guessed. They must be permitted to do pretty much what they want, and no one is allowed to stop or touch them. Having been thus anointed, they have been able to move with virtual impunity. Most of those who do get arrested by the police in the field for their criminal behavior get promptly bailed out or released. On the other hand, those who dare to oppose their radical agenda are immediately labelled as racists and all around despicable human beings. They are quickly shamed, cancelled and fired.

It is this ability to position themselves on the high moral ground that accounts for their remarkable gains. In this they follow the template that has been successfully exploited by all the great revolutionaries of the past. Robespierre, Lenin, Mao Zedong, Pol Pot, Fidel Castro and their cohorts have all claimed to be driven by lofty and noble impulses. They all managed to position themselves as the champions of the oppressed and claimed that their efforts were motivated by the desire to improve the situation of their fellow men. They also used the same basic formula to implement their destructive agendas. The formula was this: we must overthrow the existing social order in order to end oppression and bring about social and economic justice.

More than twenty-three centuries ago, Aristotle articulated a profound insight into the nature of man as a political animal: "Men start revolutionary changes for reasons connected with their private lives," he observed. What are those reasons? According to Aristotle, the motives of revolutionists are usually selfish and gross in nature. They include such base sentiments as envy and the desire for personal gain and power. We read in Book Five of his *Politics*:

> The universal and chief cause of this revolutionary feeling has been already mentioned; viz., the desire of equality, when men think that they are equal to others who have more than themselves; or, again, the desire of inequality and superiority, when conceiving themselves to be superior they think that they have not more but the same or less than their inferiors... Inferiors revolt in order that they may be equal, and equals that they may be superior. Such is the state of mind which creates revolutions. The motives for making them are the desire of gain and honor, or the fear of dishonor and loss.[44]

The truth of Aristotle's insight has been borne out by history many times since. The cost of not recognizing the true motives of revolutionists has been immense indeed. In the 20th century alone those who toppled their societies under the guises of ending oppression and bringing justice killed more than one hundred million of their fellow citizens.[45]

The question before us is this: Is the present crop of American revolutionists actuated by exalted impulses? This is the claim that has earned them license to do as they wish. Or are they motivated by the base urges of the human psyche? On the answer to this question our national and personal destinies depend.

The first red flag is their proclaimed cause. Our revolutionaries claim that the reason America's society needs to be radically remade is because of its deep-seated racism, which they call "systemic." Anyone familiar with the situation in America, however, must immediately see that this charge is bogus. Whatever faults and flaws American society may have, racism is certainly not among them. Quite to the contrary, black people in America not only enjoy complete equality with the white majority, but they have been awarded a whole set of special rights and privileges that the rest do not have.

The most frequently cited "evidence" of systemic racism is police brutality which, it is asserted, is unduly directed against black men. However, study after study has shown that cops do not target black men because of the color of their skin. In fact, when it comes to deaths in police encounters black suspects are underrepresented.

These facts notwithstanding, anti-racism activists absurdly claim that the police are committing genocide against black people. In August of this year Naomi Osaka, one of the world's top tennis players, withdrew from a tournament to protest this completely fictional issue. This is what she wrote: "Watching the continued genocide of black people at the hand of the police makes is honestly making me sick to the stomach... When will it ever be enough?"[46]

Whatever is making Osaka sick to the stomach it surely cannot be the police "genocide" of blacks, because such a thing simply does not exist. Osaka's missive, however, is instructive in showing how such delusional thinking takes hold of people's psyches: "I am exhausted of having a new hashtag pop up every few days and I am extremely tired of having this same conversation over and over again."

The tactics of the demagogues are obvious: they relentlessly keep putting out untruths on the internet, which then keep popping up on people's screens. When people see this information a hundred times, they take it to be a fact. Goethe's maxim applies now more than ever:

Truth has to be repeated constantly, because Error also is being preached all the time, and not just by a few, but by the multitude. In the Press and Encyclopaedias, in Schools and Universities, everywhere Error holds sway, feeling happy and comfortable in the knowledge of having Majority on its side.[47]

The fact is, despite what Osaka and others like her may think, white suspects are more likely to be killed by law enforcement than black suspects. Furthermore, policemen are far more likely to be killed by black men than black man to be killed by the police. Contemplate these facts cited by Heather MacDonald in her Wall Street Journal article titled "The Myth of Systemic Racism":

In 2018 there were 7,407 black homicide victims. Assuming a comparable number of victims last year, those nine unarmed black victims of police shootings represent 0.1% of all African Americans killed in 2019. By contrast, a police officer is 18½ times more likely to be killed by a black male than an unarmed black male is to be killed by a police officer.[48]

Despite their constant barrage of racism accusations and complaints, the critics cannot point to a single racist law, practice or institution. And there is a good reason for this: the notion of systemic anti-black racism in America is an utter myth.

The only institutional racism that exists in America today is racism against white and Asian people, mainly in education, government employment and contracting but in other areas of life as well. In August 2020, for example, the US Department of Justice found Yale University in violation of the civil right laws by discriminating against white and Asian students in favor of blacks. According to Reuters:

The U.S. Justice Department on Thursday accused Yale University of illegally discriminating against Asian American and white applicants in its undergraduate admissions process in violation of U.S. civil rights law.[49]

Apparently, white and Asian students have a 90 percent lower chance of being admitted than black applicants with comparable credentials. If this is not racial discrimination, what is? Yale, of course, is not alone in this. These kinds of practices are completely normal not only throughout our educational system but throughout our society. If truth be told, black people in America are the most cosseted racial minority in history. This is the reason why black people from all over the globe want to come and start their life here. As if things were not good enough already, free looting has now apparently been added to the list of special benefits and privileges that blacks in America enjoy over the rest of the population.

Other revolutionaries at least got their initial cause right. Lenin was onto something when he said that the workers and peasants were oppressed in Russia at his time. With today's American social activists, however, even their ostensible cause is thoroughly fake. But it is not only the obvious falseness of their rallying cry that should make us doubt the nobleness of their motives. It is their very demeanor and behavior. The way they scream and shout, the way they curse, their insolence and violence – all these clearly show something deeply amiss. Many people have been startled by the mugshots of arrested protestors released by the police departments across the country.

The obviously troubled individuals in these mugshots were apprehended while rioting under the cover of the noble ideal of social justice. These are the "mostly peaceful protestors" who roam our streets and terrorize innocent citizens. These are the kinds of people that Democrat politicians across the country shield from prosecution. Do you think that the kind of society these disturbed types would bring about would really be good and just?

Do you really believe that the woke and progressives are actuated by noble motives of justice and equity as they claim to be? Watching them, one cannot but feel sorry. Troubled and selfish, most of them are spoiled and disordered individuals whose moral sense has been seriously impaired by the self-indulgent, undisciplined lives they have led.

Such people are incapable of genuinely caring for the well-being of others. To truly care for other human beings – to have real empathy – one must be unselfish at least to some degree. These people are anything but that. They are not doing what they are doing for the noble reasons they cite. Swept by the dark winds of Atropos, their fight against (non-existent) racism is merely an excuse to give an expression to their hatred of the system they blame for their suffering which has been brought on by their dysfunctional lifestyles. Watching today's activists in action, the truth of Aristotle's observation becomes glaringly obvious: "Men [and women]," indeed, "start revolutionary changes for reasons connected with their private lives."

This is not to say that our society does not need change or reform, because there are a number of things have gone wrong. But there is a big difference between serious thought-out reform and a heedless revolution that sweeps everything away. The difference is that of life and death. We have seen what happened in the past when moral desperadoes gain power through revolutionary upheaval. Today's American Atropos-beholden revolutionaries want to topple our society in the name of a non-existent problem while ignoring the real ones. Their cause is false, their proposed solutions are wrong and the system they aspire to install would spell disaster for this country and its people. This is why the kind of revolution they are trying to stoke must not succeed.

THE LEFT'S WONDERLAND: TWILIGHT ZONE USA

G rowing up in a communist regime was like living in a twilight zone where everything had gone topsy-turvy. If you've never been to a twilight zone, it is a most curious phenomenon. It comes into existence when in a certain country or a geographic location a blatantly false narrative takes hold of the collective psyche.

The narrative of the leftist twilight zone of my youth went roughly as follows: socialism was the greatest socio-economic system ever devised while capitalism was very, very bad. The Soviet Union was a paradisiacal land of freedom, opportunity, prosperity and happiness. The United States, on the other hand, was a country of exploitation and oppression where most people were bound, destitute and miserable. This official narrative was constantly and relentlessly promulgated from every quarter of our twilight zone: schools, government, television, radio, arts, newspapers, magazines and so on. Needless to say, the narrative ran in complete contravention of reality. The actual truth was that socialism was no good. On the other hand, most people in the United States were free, quite prosperous and reasonably happy while the Soviet Union was pretty much an all-around hellhole.

Those who attempted to point out the truth or question the authorized storyline were promptly silenced, suppressed and punished. As a result of the swift and efficient censorship the false narrative prevailed and took a deep hold on the societal mind. And because it served as the paradigm for reality, it distorted and turned upside down almost every aspect of life: the good was bad and bad was good; white was black and black was white. The values and ethics in the twilight zone became inverted.

Escaping from behind the Iron Curtain, I thought I was done with twilight zones for good. But as I watched in amazement the events of the last few weeks, I saw something happen that I would have never dreamed possible: The American left has managed to pull the United States into a twilight zone of its own.

As with every twilight zone, America's also came into existence as the result of a false narrative. This narrative runs thus: The United States of America is a racist country in which black people are oppressed and where systemic racism prevails. In America every non-black person is racist. This applies even to those who have never done or said anything that could be conceivably construed as racist. The racism of such people is unconscious – they simply cannot see it due to their white privilege.

As with the communist narrative of old, leftists' claim that the United States is systemically racist and oppressive toward black people is completely false. This is something that should be readily obvious to every reasonable person. No society in history has, in fact, done more for the advancement and upliftment of black people than the United States of America. And this includes all of the black nations and systems that ever existed.

The obvious fact that the US is not a racist nation was actually quite evident to most people until very recently. If in the early months of 2020 someone seriously claimed that America is an institutionally racist country, he would have been viewed either as a professional race hustler or a far fringe crank. Today, however, most of the media, Big Tech, corporate and athletic establishments and officials on all levels of government are proclaiming this very thing.

Out of the countless instances, let us just mention one.

On June 5, the NFL Commissioner Roger Goodell released a communication which read in part:

> We, the NFL, condemn racism and the systematic oppression of Black People. We, the NFL, admit we were wrong for not listening to NFL players earlier and encourage all to speak out and peacefully protest. We, the NFL, believe Black Lives Matter.[50]

We are not going to comment on the vacuousness of these words. We just note the paradox of this statement being made by the highest official in the NFL, which happens to be a highly exclusive sports association of which 70 percent of players are black.[51] But such paradoxes – along with truth in general – are lost on most people these days.

The speed with which the false narrative gained hold of the American psyche is truly astounding. As the racism claim was rapidly gaining its hold on our collective mindset in June 2020, we witnessed a corresponding frenzy of accusations and kneelings, prostrations, self-flagellation and repentance of white privilege. All this took place against a backdrop of much destruction and burning cities set ablaze by the "mostly peaceful" protesters. (Who still have to explain how looting stores and stealing iPhones and Nikes furthers the cause of racial justice.)

All this drama is quite inexplicable, especially since the premise behind it is demonstrably false. It almost feels as along with COVID-19 we have also been affected by some strange malady which could only be called "faux racism." This bug gets straight in the brain and makes people say things that are not true. It is extremely communicable as evidenced by its rapid spread into every sector of our society. The contagious strain was apparently spawned under the pressure and heat of the lockdown which the left utilized to transform decades of racial demagoguery into a destructive mixture of combativeness and guilt in which all kinds of false claims and accusations flourish and thrive.

Today the bug is literally everywhere. Seeking a respite, the other day I headed over to Audible.com in hope of finding some wholesome title that would take the mind off the enveloping madness. No sooner than I landed on the homepage, I was in for a bad surprise. Right across the top of the website ran a big banner titled "Anti-racism listening list." The message below read: "The fight for racial justice is up to all of us. If you're not sure where to start, these listening recommendations can help."

Nowhere on the list could one find Thomas Sowell's excellent book Black Rednecks and White Liberals.[52] In this book, Sowell – who is a brilliant black thinker and writer – documents the immense efforts and sacrifices made by the United States and the United Kingdom to end the practice of slavery across the world. (To get an idea, you can listen to chapter three of Sowell's book on YouTube under the entry "Thomas Sowell - The Real History of Slavery." It is a veritable *tour de force*, which, I believe, will be worth your while.)

The cost to the United States of doing away with slavery in terms of effort, treasure and life was incalculable. It was on the back of this that America was able to gradually fashion a system that today gives black people more rights, resources and privileges than other societies in the history of mankind. Sadly, these days such little details and facts are not allowed into acceptable discourse. Instead, almost everyone seems to be suffering from a bad case of faux racism. Being under its spell we all now sound the same, repeat the same phrases and clichés, which ring both hollow and untrue. And the falsity of it all we either do not see it, or do not want to see it, or are afraid to admit it.

Once in its grip a person quickly becomes a shadow of his former self. We could point to many examples, but we will highlight just a couple. Recently, Mitt Romney was filmed[53] participating in one of the Black Lives Matter marches in Washington, DC. When asked why he was there, the Utah senator and former republican presidential candidate replied, "to end violence and brutality and to make sure that people understand that black lives matter." What a sad sight he was. Co-opted by a movement built on untruths, a man who once used to have a measure of stature and presence suddenly seemed very small as he discharged his empty clichés from behind his COVID mask. He almost looked like a caricature of those faceless marchers that used to come out en masse during May Day demonstrations in the Soviet Block. What happened to you, sir, one wanted to exclaim.

Or take Jacob Frey, the mayor of Minneapolis, who groveled pitifully[54] before a black woman standing over him in what looked like some open air tribunal set up by the rioters for doing away with the police. The woman confronts the mayor thus: "Jacob Frey, we have a yes or no question for you. Yes or no, will you commit to defunding Minneapolis Police Department?... We don't want no more police. Is that clear?"

The stern lady-judge is obviously unaware that by policing black neighborhoods across this nation the American law enforcement actually saves black lives. This has been shown recently by a black Harvard economist Roland Fryer who has done extensive research into the matter. You can read about this in a Wall Street Journal article aptly titled "Good Policing Saves Black Lives."[55]

But as he is questioned by the Tribunal, Mayor Frey fails to point this out. Seeing him standing there in jeans and a t-shirt, scared and confused like some errant schoolboy, one could not but feel sorry for him. Afraid to give the response they do not want to hear, he tries his best to muffle the answer behind his little mask. But the crowd would have none of his waffling – they want to hear the answer loud and clear. With a microphone stuck into his face, there is no way out. Caught between a rock and a hard place, the mayor says: "I do not support full abolition of the Minneapolis Police Department."

His words draw a firestorm of contempt and fury from the ireful crowd. "Get the f--- out of here!" he is promptly ordered. Jeered and ridiculed, he scampers away while the throng chants, "shame, go home, Jacob, go home." As the hapless mayor makes his humiliating exit, the incensed assembly continues to yell,

"Shame! Shame! Shame! Shame!..." Luckily for Frey, he manages to make off without injury although he does come very close to being physically assaulted on his way out.

As in every twilight zone, severe censorship is the order of the day. Media outlets – social and otherwise – are now patrolled by ruthless woke truth squads who immediately flag, complain about and report any view or fact that does chime with the left's official narrative. Any attempt to question it or to point to facts that show it to be untrue is immediately labelled as "offensive" "racist" "dangerous" or "a violation of the terms of use." As a result of this concentrated and relentless effort, a great amount of valuable educational material – both in the form of video and written word – has been either blocked or removed from various internet outlets and social networks. The mainstream media outlets are not helpful either, as they appear to be voluntarily self-isolating from anything that even remotely smacks of truth.

But it is not merely that facts and truth must be expunged from public discourse. As in every twilight zone, those who dare to promulgate the truth – however mildly – must be swiftly punished and penalized. Take the latest example of a Vermont High School principal by the name of Tiffany Riley. Riley was fired from her job by the school officials for posting the following message on her Facebook page:

> I firmly believe that Black Lives Matter, but I do not agree with the coercive measures taken to get this point across; some of which are falsified in an attempt to prove a point. While I want to get behind BLM, I do not think people should be made to feel they have to choose black race over human race. While I understand the urgency to feel compelled to advocate for black lives, what about our fellow law enforcement? What about all others who advocate for and demand equity for all? Just because I don't walk around with a BLM sign should not mean I am a racist.[56]

How can any sane person find anything sanction worthy in this perfectly reasonable and delicately worded expression of personal opinion? And yet at this time of extreme censorship and unbridled political correctness, making such an innocent statement cost Tiffany Riley her job.

Sadly, she is only one of many. In case you are interested, you can peruse a list of some of the people who have lost their jobs, position and reputation for expressing their views on the website, Daily Beast, under a posting titled "Everyone Who's Lost their Job During the 2020 Racism Reckoning."[57] The offences of most of the victims were as innocuous as that of Ms. Riley of Vermont. What a paradox: in the supposedly freest country on earth where free speech is protected by a constitutional amendment people are not allowed so much as to hint at the truth even in the mildest of terms.

What in the world has happened to us?

Welcome to Twilight Zone USA: courtesy of the progressive left.

DEMOCRATS' DAY OF INFAMY: THE PERNICIOUS INFLUENCE OF MULTICULTURALISM

On June 8 a group of some twenty leading Congressional Democrats – including House Speaker Nancy Pelosi and Senate Minority Leader Charles Schumer – knelt down and bowed their heads in the Emancipation Hall of the US Capitol building in Washington in DC. Contrary to appearance, the purpose of this solemnity was not to honor God. The Democrats performed this act of self-abnegation in capitulation to Black Lives Matter whose members have been pressurizing citizens of this country to kneel down in acknowledgment of their claims and grievances. Black Lives Matter (BLM) is a Marxist organization that claims that America is an irredeemably racist and unjust society that oppresses black people. Because of this deeply rooted racism, BLM insists, American institutions and ways of doing things must be torn down and replaced with a new order. To make this point clear, BLM has organized and spearheaded riots across the country that attacked symbols of American culture and destroyed dozens of cities. The burning of the American flag and chants of "F-ck America!" have been commonplace at such events. In one of their recent rallies the protestors also chanted "F-ck your Jesus!" It is truly difficult to see the relevance of this blasphemous obscenity except as the nihilistic desire to desecrate anything and everything that has to do with this country's history and heritage.

Needless to say, the claims of BLM are completely false. America is not a racist society. Not only do black people in America have the same rights as the white majority, they enjoy special rights and privileges (to which looting privileges are the latest addition) that the rest do not. The list of these is long and we have already covered the subject elsewhere. For now, let us just mention the special quotas for minorities in government employment and contracts as well as in university admissions. Only last month the US Department of Justice found that a major IVY league university is in violation of civil rights laws by illegally discriminating[58]in its admission procedures against white and Asian students in favor of blacks. This is nothing but an unseemly form of racism, but this racism is certainly not directly against black candidates. Such pro-black discriminatory practices are common throughout the American system of higher education as well as in other spheres of life.

The Democrats' kneeling ceremony was ostensibly conducted in memory of George Floyd, a violent serial criminal whose death has been advertised as evidence of racism in America. It is racism, they say, that inspired the act of police excess that resulted in Floyd's death. But within days of the incident there was already a large body of evidence that clearly showed that Floyd's demise occurred as a result of drug overdose. The autopsy [59] by the medical examiner revealed no signs of trauma to his torso or to his breathing apparatus, proving that Floyd was not killed by the cop who held him. George Floyd died due to a cardiopulmonary arrest brought on by a lethal dose of Fentanyl in his system which was two times the fatal level. (If you are interested, we recommend an excellent analysis[60]of the issue in an article written by John Leonard titled *"Or Did George Floyd Die of a Drug Overdose?* The article is available on the internet and includes links to relevant primary sources.) The reason Floyd was put into hold was because the policemen on the scene correctly determined that he was suffering from excited delirium (EXD). Excited delirium is an episode of violent agitation caused by drug overdose. This burst of energy often takes place moments before death occurs. Even as the officers placed Floyd under restraint, they phoned for an ambulance. They did exactly what they were supposed to do. They subdued the fatally overdosed man in the grip of excited delirium and called for medical assistance in an effort to save his life.

By kneeling in the Capitol on June 8, the Democrats accepted the slanderous accusations against their own nation. This was truly a moment of infamy when leaders of a major US political party surrendered before the false claims of a radical Atropic organization whose stated goal is the toppling of American society as we know it. In a truly strange twist to this event, even as the Democrats showed contempt for their own nation's heritage, they draped themselves in a symbol of a foreign culture. As they were kneeling with their heads bowed colorful shawls hung from their shoulders. They were made of so-called Kente cloth. In case you do not know what it is, here is some background information from a fact checking outfit called Politifact:

> The first Kente cloth emerged about 500 years ago in the area of West Africa now known as Ghana. The dominant group were the Ashanti, who, by the early 1800s, controlled nearly all of the area of present-day Ghana (Asante is an alternative spelling.)... The Ashanti played a well-documented role in the European slave trade. In the 1700s, millions of Africans passed through Ghana ports, having been sold to British and Dutch slavers in exchange for weapons and other European goods. The British abolished slavery in 1807, but enforcement of the ban in Western Africa was weak.[61]

What a paradox! Even as they honored the specious charge

of racism against their own country, the Democrats wrapped themselves in a symbol of a slave trading society. The Asante were black people, which means that they preyed on other black people whom they captured and sold by shipload to whoever paid the best price. Perhaps the Democrats may want to know what the Asante did with their ill-gotten gains. According to an article in the USA Today:

> The Asante supplied British and Dutch traders with slaves in exchange for firearms, which they used to expand their empire. Slaves were often acquired as tributes from smaller states or captured during war. Some slaves were brought across the Atlantic whiles others stayed in Africa to work in gold fields.[62]

So, with the profits obtained by selling out their African compatriots, the Asante bought firearms which they used to murder more black Africans in their rapacious conquests. It must have been a sorry sight indeed. Since in the 18th century the native African civilization was only in an early iron age stage of development, the black people whom the Asante aimed to subdue were armed only with primitive weapons. The firearms gave the Asante an overwhelming advantage which these ruthless people exploited to the full. The lead bullets from their newly acquired rifles easily mowed down their virtually defenseless victims armed with bows, spears, sticks and stones.

Worse yet, the Asante never repented and only rolled back their slave trade when the Westerners banned the practice. The Asante, however, would not let go lightly. Their attitude seems to be typical of indigenous African cultures, all of which seem to have been deeply steeped in slavery, oppression and cruelties of different kinds such as misogyny as well as human sacrifice. In fact, misogyny, female circumcision, slavery and human trafficking are practiced in many places in Africa to this very day in spite of two centuries of Western efforts to stop these kinds of barbaric practices. Unbelievably, indigenous African cultures continue to practice child sacrifice to this day. From Wikipedia:

> In Sub-Saharan Africa, "the practice of ritual killing and human sacrifice continues to take place ... in contravention of the African Charter on Human and Peoples' Rights and other human rights instruments." In the 21st century, such practices have been reported in Nigeria, Uganda, Swaziland, Liberia, Tanzania, Namibia, and Zimbabwe, as well as Mozambique, and Mali. This is the harmful practice of removing body parts, blood or tissue from a child who is still alive.[63]

The Asante's history of oppression, slave-trading and murder should draw a special kind of condemnation in these racially sensitive times when statues of those who had even the most tangential connection to slavery are being desecrated. Rather than covering themselves in symbols of black slavery, the leftists in the US Congress should push for a special resolution condemning the unwholesome deeds of the Asante people – as well as other African slave-trading tribes – who not only enslaved their fellow Africans but never apologized or expressed regret for their actions. Have these Congressional Democrats no shame? If they had any sense of justice, they would – instead of parading themselves in Kente shawls – travel to Africa and pull down the statues of all Asante chieftains as well non-chieftains, since that culture was so deeply enmeshed in slavery that no man was innocent of it.

The Democrats' Kente cloth antics are the result of moral confusion sown by four decades of multiculturalism. Multiculturism, as you may know, is the destructive Atropos inspired ideology that slanders and denigrates Western culture while extolling the alleged virtues of foreign and exotic cultures such as the spirit-worshiping,[64] slave-trading Asante. How astonishing that while denigrating their own legacy the Congressional Democrats would voluntarily wear insignia of such a predatory people. What have the Asante ever done for the good of mankind to merit such an honor in the halls of the US Capitol? If the historical records are anything to go by, their main legacy seems to be slavery, chicanery and misogyny.

The Democrats' own country's contributions to the well-being of humanity, on the other hand, are immense. For one thing, America has created a truly free and affluent society. In America the descendants of the Asante as well as the progeny of those whom they enslaved and sold off not only enjoy equal rights with the white majority, but they even receive special privileges. This by itself would be a great accomplishment, but it is only one of many. America has also been the last hope of man as it led the world in the struggle against the dark forces of fascism and communism. Over the last one hundred and fifty years, Americans have gifted the world with tremendous discoveries and advancement across most fields of human endeavor. Science, technology, education have all been blessed by the efforts of resourceful and industrious Americans. They have sent men to the moon and tackled the frontiers of space. They have created life-saving medicines and technologies. America has given us the automobile, the lightbulb, the washing machine, the motion picture, the airplane, the transistor, Coca Cola, the microchip, the Levi jeans, the microwave, the internet, the Hubble Space Telescope, the personal computer, Elvis and the iPhone among many other things. It has also given us Donald Duck, McDonald's and now even the Donald himself.

What have the Asante accomplished in the meantime? What are their contributions to the advancement of humanity? Where are their inventions? We have yet to see the Asante equivalent of the space shuttle, but a humble radio receiver would also do.

The Democrats' Asante stunt brings to mind the antics of another hapless Atropic "leader." He was a Roman emperor by the name Gratian who ascended to power in 375 AD. Like today's Democrats, he found himself at the helm of his country at a time of crisis when the Roman empire was facing severe pressures on multiple fronts. Like the Democrats, Gratian was also apparently an avid multiculturalist. The wretched emperor surrounded himself with members of foreign tribes with whom he would spend much of his time. As with the Democrats' enthusiasm for the Asante, Gratian seems to have had a special liking for the Alans, a barbaric tribe from behind the Rhine River. He gave them official positions and – like the Democrats on the Capitol Hill the other day – he would appear in court decked out in their exotic garb. This promotion of foreign pagans angered his Christian army and caused revulsion among decent patriotic Romans. They tried to bear with their foolish emperor for a while but when his incompetence became unbearable, they had him cancelled.

It is hoped that the treacherous Democrats will get cancelled by the ballot box at the next election. But we should not hold our breath. The decades of relentless multiculturalism have wrought their insidious work. When our culture is being denigrated and destroyed, there are few left to defend it.

TRUTH ABOUT AMERICA: WHY WE ARE NOT A RACIST NATION

"Racism in America is not the exception – it's the norm,"[65] read a headline from the British Guardian the other day.

"2 viruses -- COVID and racism -- devastate the black community and threaten America's stability,"[66] declares an ABC News piece.

"Not just George Floyd: Police departments have 400-year history of racism,"[67] headlines an USA Today article.

A great deal, indeed, has been recently said about the alleged oppressiveness and racism of American society. Even though these denunciations have been delivered in impassioned voices and accompanied by much violence, there is one problem with such claims: they are not true.

The fact is that there is no institutional or systemic discrimination against black people in American society. Contrary to the assertions we hear today, in the last half a century America has gone into untold lengths to support and assist its black community. During this time, American society has launched countless programs and initiatives and spent hundreds of billions of dollars aimed specifically at uplifting the African American demographic. The support that the black community receives from American society comes in every form conceivable: legislative, financial, educational, commercial, human, material.

To ensure that there is no systemic or institutional discrimination, America went so far as to implement affirmative action and racial quotas in education, employment, government contracts, housing and other areas of life. This means that our laws and codes of conduct grant more protection, privileges and guarantees to colored people than they do to their white counterparts. So eager and willing has America been to elevate its black minority that it actually subjected the majority to reverse discrimination. To redeem itself and correct a legacy of past discrimination, the United States has bent backwards to advance its black population. The amount of resources, protection and goodwill that America's black minority receives from our society is completely unprecedented in the annals of world history.

Nowhere in the world do black people enjoy more freedom and greater financial, employment and educational opportunities than they do in the United States. This is the reason why so many black people from all over the globe seek to come and live in this country. Such great are their numbers that we can only accept a tiny fraction of those who wish to come here. If America was such a racist and oppressive nation, why would they want to come so badly?

The reason they want to come is because they know that America treats black people well and that nowhere else in the world do black people have it as good as they have it here. When black people whose vision has not been distorted by the demagoguery of the so-called civil rights leaders look at America, they see freedom and opportunity. They look at America and see a country that has recently awarded the most coveted and prestigious job in the world – the presidency of the United States – to a black man. And this not once, but two times. Would a racist nation ever do something like that?

Despite all the criticism, we never hear stories of African Americans leaving this "racist" "oppressive" country and then returning with tales of lands where black people lead lives of more abundance and dignity. Have you ever heard such a testimony? Let us see one country in the world that is more generous and caring towards blacks than this one. Let us find one nation which affords black people more freedom and protection than the United States of America. Tellingly, we cannot find a single predominantly black country where its citizens enjoy more rights and affluence than the black people in the United States. Isn't it paradoxical that the United States treats its black people better than black nations treat their own? The immense lengths – involving both effort and treasure – into which this society has gone to help and accommodate black Americans are surely worth pondering. In a healthy society, this would draw at least sporadic expressions of gratitude and appreciation.

If truth be told, African Americans are the most favored and legally privileged demographic in American society. Enjoying the benefits of a host of protective measures and mechanisms incorporated into the fabric of our societal existence, African Americans are neither systemically oppressed nor are they institutionally discriminated against. An eye-opening expression of this took place last June during the "anti-racism" protests in Washington, DC. There a local black woman by the named Nestride Yumga confronted a group of protesters promulgating their stock racist slogans against this country. In the course of the exchange, the woman chastises a white protestor:

> You say blacks are oppressed. I am black and I am not oppressed. I am free!... Stop forcing on people to accept that they are oppressed... You are forcing a rhetoric into their minds which is not true... Shame on you, I am free![68]

Standing in front of them with outstretched arms, Nestride's words have a stunning effect that leaves the startled demonstrators groping for a reply. The impact of her utterance is so powerful, because what she says is so obviously and undeniably true. Unlike the rioters and protestors we see shouting untruths from our screens, this young black woman truly speaks truth to power. And what a power hers is. Turning toward the black members of the crowd, she excoriates them, "You guys are not oppressed. You are lazy, that's all it is. Go get jobs, work!"

Blindsided by this unexpected petard of stark truth, the dazed demonstrators weakly attempt a couple of hollow clichés and some heckling by way of response. Hit with such a healthy dose of reality, they are unable to mount any kind of coherent answer. The black woman's reproof rips off the cloak of righteous falsehood from their faux cause of racism and they stand there exposed, clutching pitiably to the shreds of their specious lies. Befuddled and confused, they pack up their protest paraphernalia and decamp. As they retreat, the intrepid lady sends them on their way with her last salvo "you guys have been cowards."

But what about the allegations police brutality against black Americans, of which the George Floyd incident is falsely used as evidence? As Tucker Carlson noted recently on his program, in 2019 ten unarmed African Americans were shot dead by police officers in the United States.[69] Nine of them had serious criminal records. On the other hand, less than two weeks ago on May 31, 2020, eighteen black people were murdered in the city of Chicago by mostly black criminals.[70] More black people are thus shot and killed by black people in one day in one city than they are killed by the police across the United States in one whole year. The allegations that are these days levelled of the police committing "black genocide" are thus utterly absurd. As Theodore Dalrymple points out a "policeman is about fifteen times more likely to be killed by a black man than to kill a black man."[71] And most of the small number of black men killed annually by the police are dangerous felons who are killed in the process of committing a crime.

Moreover, more white people are shot by the police than black people,[72] and likewise more white people die in arrest-related incidents than black people.[73] The narrative that the police routinely round up innocent peaceful black men in the streets is a complete myth that no one in their right mind can believe, not least black people themselves. According to Pew research, more than half of black Americans have "a lot" or at least "some" confidence in the police. As a point of comparison, less than one third of the American population approve of the way Congress is handling its job. In other words, far more black people have confidence in their local cops that we have in our elected representatives in Washington, DC. Most upright black Americans want our law enforcement and government officials take a strong stance against lawlessness no matter by whom it is perpetrated. The latest evidence of this is Donald Trump's record approval rating among likely black voters in the wake of the riots.[74] Tellingly, Donald Trump has been one of the few government figures who has not pandered to the looting mobs.

The question, then, is: given all the financial, legislative, educational and human resources that have been poured into the black community over the decades, why is the black community not thriving? Why, after all these years of immense effort and investment, is the black community still plagued with so many difficulties?

The answer is not racism, police brutality or discrimination. The troubles of the black community are mostly due to the moral breakdown within its ranks, especially in the inner cities.

Data shows that more than seventy five percent of black babies are born to single mothers.[75] And from those 25 percent who are born to parents who are married fewer still grow up to adulthood with both of their biological parents present. This means that the majority of young black people grow up in broken or dysfunctional homes. In any racial demographic that by itself would be a problem with catastrophic consequences. And the statistics are, indeed, devastating.[76] Consider some of the following facts. Children from fatherless families are five times more likely to grow up in poverty and commit crime. Children from father-absent homes are nearly three times more likely to carry guns and deal drugs than those living with their fathers. They are also nine times more likely to drop out of school. Worse yet, young people from broken families are 20 times more likely to go to prison.

As far back as 1965, Daniel Patrick Moynihan warned that the destruction of the black nuclear family would have ruinous economic and social consequences for the black community. When Moynihan was writing his famous report the black illegitimacy rate was 25 percent.[77] Today it is three times higher.

Sadly, the destruction of the black nuclear family has been to a great extent facilitated by government which creates incentives for this by providing cash payments and an array of benefits to single mothers. "The steady expansion of welfare programs can be taken as a measure of the steady disintegration of the Negro family structure over the past generation in the United States," wrote Moynihan in the conclusion to his paper.

The black writer Larry Elder recalls a story of some years ago when he interviewed Kweisi Mfume who was at the time president of the National Association for the Advancement of Colored People (NAACP). In the course of the interview, Elder posed this question: "Between the presence of white racism and the absence of black fathers which poses the bigger threat to the black community?" Without any hesitation, Mfume replied, "the absence of black fathers."

Bad as this is, for many black children growing up in dysfunctional families this in itself is not the end of difficulties. Most of them also live immersed in a culture and mindset that makes it virtually impossible to pursue happy and meaningful existence. It is truly regrettable that black street culture promotes and celebrates gross human traits and forms of conduct. Sexual promiscuity, illegitimacy, violence, instant gratification, drug abuse, indolence and crime are celebrated and held up as if they were virtues. On the other hand, those who by studiousness, uprightness and work ethic try to escape the hopeless existence that such a view of life inevitably engenders are accused of "acting white" and derided as Uncle Toms and Aunt Annas. How absurd. Those who make such derisory statements seem to imply that living an upright and conscientious life is a racial trait that should only be displayed by white people.

What hope can there be for young people growing up in broken homes – which are often negligent and abusive – while being submerged in such a toxic culture? We see the tragic result in the looting mobs that are vandalizing and burning American cities today. The pandemonium they have unleashed is not the consequence of white racism or police brutality. It is the inevitable outcome of the illegitimacy, broken culture and moral decline that has unraveled the moral fiber of large swathes of the black demographic.

What the black community needs at this time is not more protests, money or government programs. What it needs is a moral rebirth and a return to the values of personal responsibility, discipline and honest work. This is where the real problem lies and unless it is addressed and faced squarely, the black community will never escape the pathologies and difficulties it is presently struggling with.

THE TRUTH ABOUT THE WEST: IT'S THE ONLY NON-OPPRESSIVE CIVILIZATION

Hey, hey, ho, ho, Western Civ has got to go.
— Jesse Jackson

"Western Civilization is not, for me, a curriculum of democracy and reason and greatness; it is a history of inequality and oppression," writes Scott Ross, a teacher, on his blog. Mr. Ross is by no means a rare ideological outlier among his peers. The view he holds has been taught and propagated at universities across the United States and Western Europe for decades. The situation has become so dire that Yale University has recently cancelled its formerly excellent course called "Introduction to Art History: Renaissance to the Present," because it was allegedly too Eurocentric.[78] Some among the shrinking number of universities that still offer such courses use them merely as a platform to attack the very culture whose achievements they are supposed to teach. The alleged oppressiveness of the West is the leitmotif that dominates their critiques. This view has boiled over into the larger society and is vigorously advocated by the Atropos-beholden political Left, which is determined to do away with Western values and ways. We have seen a disturbing display of this mindset during the recent riots when "protesters" kept methodically attacking and destroying symbols of Western culture.

Although it is true that various forms of oppression have been practiced in the West over time, oppression is by no means unique to the West. Oppression has been, in fact, a feature of every civilization that has appeared on the face of this earth. We could say that human history is – in one way – a history of oppression: it has been common for those with power to exploit, trample upon and take advantage of their fellow human beings. There is nothing particularly surprising about this, since selfishness and rapaciousness are prominent aspects of human nature.

What makes the West unique, however, is that it is the only civilization to reject oppression and deem it both wrong and immoral. Western civilization stands as the only culture that has had the compassion and humanness to make a deliberate and systematic effort to eliminate oppression and tyranny not only from within its own territories but also in other parts of the world. Central to this enterprise has been the concept of human rights. It was Western thinkers who came up with the unprecedented and novel idea that all men (and women) are entitled to certain fundamental inalienable rights which they possess simply by virtue of being human.

This is how Encyclopedia Wikipedia sums up the evolution of this revolutionary concept:

> Ancient peoples did not have the same modern-day conception of universal human rights. The true forerunner of human rights discourse was the concept of natural rights which appeared as part of the medieval natural law tradition that became prominent during the European Enlightenment with such philosophers as John Locke, Francis Hutcheson and Jean-Jacques Burlamaqui which featured prominently in the political discourse of the American Revolution and the French Revolution. From this foundation, the modern human rights argu-

ments emerged over the latter half of the 20th century possibly as a reaction to slavery, torture, genocide and war crimes, as a realisation of inherent human vulnerability and as being a precondition for the possibility of a just society.[79]

Please note carefully: the concept of universal human rights was developed wholly and exclusively within the Western Tradition. Some of the landmark public declarations where this singularly Western principle has been annunciated include the American Constitution and the Bill of Rights, The Declaration of the Rights of Man, and the United Nations' Universal Declaration of Human Rights. No other civilization has had the inclination and generosity to extend such rights to the common man. Most of them have, in fact, strongly resisted this kind of developments in the past, and they still do so today.

Universal human rights are a quintessentially Western project. The idea that the king and the pauper, the great and the small, the rich and the poor have the same intrinsic worth and as such are entitled to the same considerations and privileges is not only uniquely western but also inimical to the mindset of every other civilizational stream. Thankfully, Western civilization did not stay with theory only. Over the centuries it has managed – with fits and starts – to evolve a system of governance which translated its lofty ideals into social reality. This achievement has been effected through a form of government which is today known as Western democracy.

According to Encyclopedia Wikipedia, the characteristic feature of Western democracy is "equal protection of human rights, civil rights, civil liberties and political freedoms for all people."[80] This is a reasonably fair and accurate description of this distinctly Western form of government. Notice especially the phrase "all people," which means every person regardless of their social standing, gender, race, creed or sexual orientation.

Thanks to their highly evolved institutions built on respect for the inherent dignity of the individual, Western democracies treat all people equally before the law and protect the rights of all people regardless of their status or accidents of birth. To ensure maximum fairness, western societies take special care to protect the civil rights of those who belong to groups that have historically found themselves at increased risk of oppression. By instituting the rule of law and guaranteeing the equality of rights, Western democracy has for the first time in history relieved the common man from his long burden of oppression. Having suffered millennia of domination and tyranny, ordinary people fortunate enough to live in Western style democracies can be free at last.

Not only has the West succeeded in eliminating tyranny and extending equal rights to all, it is the only civilization that has seriously attempted to embark on such an enterprise. In all other civilizations, human rights and privileges were the domain of only the privileged few. And those privileged few were invariably black, brown and yellow males, depending on the geographic location of the civilization in question. It apparently rarely occurred to these men that other classes of people in their societies may also be entitled to the same rights and considerations they themselves enjoyed. Instead, they treated the rest of the population as objects to be used and exploited for their own benefit and pleasure. And more often than not, those powerful black, brown and yellow males exercised their power over their fellow men (and women) with considerable selfishness and ruthlessness. That's why tyranny, systemic oppression, exploitation, abuse, and discrimination have always been part and parcel of every civilization save for the sole bright exception of the West. It seems that among all privileged male classes across racial groups, it was only white men who possessed the sufficient empathy and compassion to consider their fellow human being worthy of the same rights they themselves felt entitled to.

Perhaps the best way to quickly illustrate the immense difference between the West and other civilizational streams is to contrast the situation of some classes of people in Western liberal democracies with their counterparts who live in societies based on nonwestern values.

In some Islamic countries, for example, women are still forced to wear hijabs and burqas and are known to be raped as punishment for refusing to cover themselves. These women cannot walk by themselves in the street, open a bank account or own property. In Saudi Arabia women were only recently allowed to drive a car. In certain Muslim countries women are not allowed to get proper education.

In contrast consider this statistic from the United States:

Women, as a percentage of college degrees: 56%
Women, as a percentage of medical school students: 50.5%
Women, as a percentage of law school students: 51.3%[81]

In a number of African countries, where the influence of indigenous African civilization is still strong, women are subjected to female circumcision. There are no known health benefits to this practice which in many cases results in severe complications and side effects. The primary purpose behind this procedure is apparently to deprive women of the possibility of experiencing sexual pleasure. Thus, these unfortunate African women are reduced to being sexual objects for the pleasure of men and receptacles for their sperm as child bearers.

This, sadly, is only one of the cruel habits of traditional African culture which has been decidedly male-dominated and misogynistic. From the accounts we have, it is quite obvious that African civilization has for the most part treated women as chattel with females seen as objects to be bartered and used for the benefit of men. An account by a sympathetic 19th century explorer provides a painful insight into the degrading manner in which women were treated in traditional African civilization:

> The females, and especially the young ones are kept principally among the old men, who barter away their daughters, sisters or nieces, in exchange for wives for themselves or their sons. Wives are considered the absolute property of the husband, and can be given away,

or exchanged, or lent, according to his caprice ... Female children are betrothed usually from early infancy ... little real affection consequently exists between husbands and wives, a young man values a wife principally for her services as a slave.[82]

The slave-like status of women in African culture contrasts sharply with the view of women held in the West. Even as African women were being treated in the most degrading manner, Madame de Stael was one of the most admired intellectual voices in Europe, writing books and hosting literary salons in Paris. Keep in mind the picture of the tyrannized African women as you read this description of Madame de Stael: "Known as a witty and brilliant conversationalist, often dressed in daring outfits, she stimulated the political and intellectual life of her times. Her works, whether novels, travel literature or polemics, emphasized individuality and passion made a lasting mark on European thought."[83] One cannot but feel a profound admiration for a civilization that would allow a woman to rise to this level of intellectual and social preeminence at the time when nearly all other cultures would view women as intrinsically useless save for their function as household vassals and sex objects.

More than fifteen hundred years before Madame de Stael, women in ancient Rome were already allowed to inherit property, own assets, initiate a divorce and leave a will. In contrast, many African societies continue to treat their women to this day in their characteristic misogynistic fashion despite the West's long- term attempts to improve their situation. Islamic and African civilizations, however, are not alone in their degrading and oppressive treatment of women. Unfortunately, more often than not this has been the norm in almost every non-western culture. It is as sad as it is revealing that no non-western culture would of its accord extend full human, civil and political rights to their women. The improvements that they have made on this front are almost wholly due to western pressure and influence.

Turning to another group, gay people face the most severe

forms of persecution and oppression in non-western societies. In Islamic Iran, for instance, homosexuals are routinely hanged.

In South Africa homosexual women are regularly subjected to "corrective" rape and often killed by men who justify their actions by appealing to the values of indigenous African culture.

Racism and ethnic hatred are to this day the common features of the non-western frame of mind. Not only that, but most of them lack the moral framework to see that there is something fundamentally wrong with their intolerant attitudes toward people who do not look like them. We see harrowing manifestations of this in African countries which still suffer from the unfortunate influence of the indigenous mindset. The Rwandan genocide, for example, in which some eight hundred thousand people were slaughtered in 100 days, was driven by ethnic hatred of one group of black people against another.[84] Tellingly, the genocide was accompanied by gender violence. According to a UN report, "Rape was the rule and its absence was the exception... Rape was systematic and was used as a weapon."[85] Experts estimate that between 250,000 and 500,000 women were raped during the Rwandan genocide. This kind of cruelty has apparently been a common feature of the African past. The situation began to improve with the arrival of western values, but the deep-rooted tendencies of African cultures are slow to change.

We could go on, but these examples suffice. Nearly all societies based on non-western values exhibit multiple forms of oppression often to a brutal degree. Racist, intolerant, rights-denying, gay-hanging and misogynist though they may be, these cultures would treat its citizens even more oppressively had it not been for the beneficial influence of the West, which has gone to great lengths in its effort to extend the rights and dignity of people world over.

One of the steps in this effort has been the United Nation's Universal Declaration of Human Rights.[86] Seen by many as one of the loftiest expressions of the human spirit, it seeks to ensure that all societies and cultures fully respect the rights and dignity of their people. Would you like to guess the name of the only civilization whose values and ideas could give rise to this kind of document? The opening clause gives the game away: "Whereas recognition of the inherent dignity and of the equal and inalienable rights of all members of the human family is the foundation of freedom, justice and peace in the world..."

Where have we heard language like this before? "The equal and inalienable rights," "the inherent dignity," these are, of course, unmistakably western concepts. And so is the idea of freedom and justice for all. Unfortunately, many non-western cultures still resist the spirit embodied in the Declaration. Unlike Western democracies, their social systems are designed to protect the rights and privileges of the powerful few so that they can continue in their oppression, chicanery and exploitation.

It is truly paradoxical that those who charge the West with being oppressive often in the same breath express admiration for non-western cultures, almost all of which grossly violate human rights of their people and often subject them to procedures that can only be described as barbaric. This glaring contradiction betrays the critics' true motives and shows that their attack on the West – which is the only civilization willing and capable of producing free and non-oppressive societies – is completely disingenuous. Rather than seeking justice for all people, their criticism is motivated by ideological reasons that has little to do with the reality of the situation on the ground.

The charge that Western culture is inherently oppressive is one of the most ludicrous and self-refuting absurdities of this woke era. Contrary to what the leftist critics contend, the West is the only civilization that has managed to develop a system of laws, rules, customs and institutions that have made the elimination of oppression possible. The consideration and respect that the West has shown for the dignity and autonomy of ordinary human beings has no precedent or equal in world history. While the histories of other civilizations are for the most part catalogues of chicanery and tyranny, the West is the only culture that bucked and reversed that trend. Western civilization towers alone as the great rights-endowing liberator of humanity. For that, the common man (and the common woman) owe the West an eternal debt of gratitude.

LOVE OF ANCESTORS AND AMERICAN HISTORY

In the past few weeks we have watched the widespread vandalization of statues and memorials dedicated to men who played a pivotal role in the story of our nation. Among the targets were such giants of American history as George Washington, Thomas Jefferson, Andrew Jackson, Abraham Lincoln and Ulysses S. Grant.

This purge was carried out on the charge of racism. Something, however, just did not add up. A number of the men whose statues were desecrated were well ahead of their time in their views of race and they did much to further the cause of black people. But the vandals would hear none of it, which came as a surprise to many. There is, however, nothing surprising about their actions once we understand that they are driven by Atropos, the civilizational death drive.

What the statue slayers really want has nothing to do with racism. Their goal is not to fight or remedy racial injustice, which in the US has been done decades ago. Their goal is to tear America apart. The way they attempt to achieve this is quite insidious: they seek to make us ashamed of our history which, they maintain, is one of continual racism that persists to this day.

Once we internalize this spurious narrative, we cannot but repudiate our past. The moment this happens we become doomed as a nation, since no people can survive as a national entity without the intuition of togetherness which a sense of shared history helps to foster. It is precisely for this reason that all healthy countries preserve and honor the landmarks of their past, especially those dedicated to the men who played key roles at crucial junctions of their national story. It is this collective sense of history that binds a people together and gives them a feeling of belonging to a larger polity, which we call a nation. When the glue of a mutually shared past loses its binding power, a nation will, sooner or later, come apart.

This is exactly what the Atropos-inspired, internal haters of America seek to bring about. By claiming that the key players in America's history were racists, they try to portray our past as a tale of injustice. Needless to say, their charge of racism is as both misplaced and unjustified. Slavery, which they position at center of their narrative as America's original sin, has existed throughout the world since the advent of society and probably even before that. It is only relatively recently, in historical terms, that this practice has been largely relinquished.

The United States has paid a greater price in blood and treasure than any other nation to stop this practice and eliminate racism from its institutions. It did it so well that in the second half of the 20th century America's black population enjoyed more rights, opportunities and freedoms than black people in any other country at any point in history.

The claims of the statue topplers that America's past is somehow uniquely egregious because of slavery betray a lack of historical perspective. If we should condemn American history because it has been marked by this practice, then we would have to condemn almost ALL of history. In nearly all great civilizations of the past – Egypt, Sumeria, Babylon, Phoenicia, Greece, Rome, etc. – slavery was commonly practiced. In fact, these civilizations were to a great extent built on slave labor.

Should we damn them all? Are we going to say there was nothing good in them and discard their immense contributions to the advancement of mankind? Are we going to tear down statues of Plato, Aristotle, Pericles, Julius Caesar, Augustus, Cicero, and Marcus Aurelius because all of them either owned slaves or directly benefited from their labor? Are we going to condemn Jesus who lived at a time when slavery was widespread and yet chose not to launch a crusade against it? When asked how people should behave toward their Roman overlords, he stated, "Render unto Caesar what is Caesar's." He said this even though slavery was endemic in Roman society.

Until relatively recently, nearly every society or historical figure was – by the logic of today's crusaders – "tainted" by slavery in one way or another. In Europe, for instance, serfdom, which was essentially a soft form of slavery, lasted in many places well into the 18th century. In some parts of the globe such practices lasted beyond that time. In fact, slavery exists in a number of places in the world to this day. Most of those places are in Africa and most of the enslavers as well as the enslaved are black. One wonders why today's racism crusaders do not focus their attention where the real problem is.

In any case, we cannot judge history by the standards of today's woke which is a luxury that comes with our modern cushioned existence. Given slavery's historical ubiquity, it is obvious that there existed strong natural tendencies toward it as an institution. Neither was slavery seen as uniformly negative or injurious to those subjected to it. Sad though it may sound, for many in the past slavery was preferable to the alternatives they faced in life. Many people sold themselves or their children to slavery voluntarily, because they simply could not make ends meet. Furthermore, when in past wars armies were defeated and prisoners taken, there were often only two options for those on the losing side: death or servitude. Many a prisoner was glad of the availability of the latter.

As far as American history goes, it is nothing like the haters say it is. No person or country is perfect, and every person and country has committed their share of errors. America is no exception. This being said, America's has an inspiring and magnificent national narrative. America's is a history of a brave people who made a perilous voyage across the ocean in search of a new home. It is a history of those who faced very difficult conditions and managed to survive despite the odds. It is a history of a people who from humble beginnings managed to build the most prosperous and free nation the world has ever seen. Ours is a history of a young nation which after many struggles, errors and setbacks managed to build a society which translated into reality the noblest aspirations of the human soul: equality and freedom for all, white, black, yellow and everything in between. The efforts of our forefathers eventually made America a shining city on the global hill, a magnet for people from all over the world regardless of the color of their skin. That's the true essence of the American story.

The miracle of America has come about because of the dedication, strength and ingenuity of our ancestors who overcame immense challenges to make their country a better place for those would come after them. All of us – including the ungrateful complainers of today – are the fortunate beneficiaries of their sweat and blood and we should be deeply grateful for their efforts. We should be thankful regardless of our race, because America is a fair land and a land of opportunity for those willing to apply themselves.

But nothing is apparently good enough for the self-righteous critics who spit not only on the memory of our ancestors but also on everything that is good and noble. Blinded by ill-will born of their own misguided ways, they condemn America's past generations who laid the foundation for the most affluent and racially accommodating country in history. And even while living in the most institutionally unprejudiced society in the world, the critics still claim that it is "systemically" racist. The fact that they fail to submit any good evidence for their allegations is of no consequence to them.

For brats like this, nothing will ever be good enough. Put to shame by the nobility of the great men who came before them, they stand as boors next to the grand souls whose memorials they seek to desecrate. Spoiled, self-indulgent and crass, these people could never build or create a great nation, or anything worthy for that matter. All they can do is to scream, criticize, loot and destroy. Instead of trying to better themselves and make their own contribution to the great story of America, they tear down what the generations before them built with so much effort and sacrifice.

By any historical standard or measure, we Americans are very fortunate to have had great forefathers. We must not allow the ransackers and assorted malcontents to cast false aspersions on their memory. We must not let them besmirch our history by their distorted interpretations of it, because if we give up our past we will surely lose our nation. We owe a deep debt of gratitude to generations past, and we must not let anyone sever the bond of love that many of us feel towards them. Above all, to be the worthy heirs of our forefathers we must not become intimidated by the screeching of the agitators. Instead, we need to strengthen our resolve to keep defending and fighting for what we know is right. Let those who come after us say that our generation rose to the challenge and that we did it well.

ABOUT THOSE DEAD WHITE AND BLACK MALES

"Students upset by the focus on 'dead white males' demanded that the freshman course be replaced with one more inclusive toward women, minorities, and non-Western cultures."[87] Thus read a Boston Globe report about a controversy at Stanford in which students rebelled against their university's Western Culture requirement. It did not take long for Jesse Jackson to get in on the act. It was during the Stanford controversy that he first sounded his famous chant "Hey hey, ho ho, Western Culture's got to go!" Like the students he supported, Jackson, too, thought that it was wrong for universities to give so much attention to dead white males. Sad to say, in the end Stanford did yield to the protestors' demands.

This was more than two decades ago, and things have only gotten worse since. Perhaps you have also noticed that dead white males have not been getting good PR in recent years. Ceaselessly portrayed as predatorial, dominating and oppressive, they have been painted as the villains of world history. Their crowning sin was the creation of a socio-economic system – Western civilization – which they used, it is alleged, as the self-serving means for their own advancement, benefit and pleasure. This they accomplished by oppressing everyone else in their society such as women, homosexuals, racial minorities, transsexuals and whatever other identity groups or genders are yet to be discovered. Patriarchal, domineering and insensitive, dead white males exploited not only every other demographic within their own societies but also people of other cultures. So goes the official politically correct narrative of our times. The widespread attacks on the symbols of western culture which we witnessed in recent months is the logical culmination of this line of thought.

We have argued earlier that this characterization may not be quite correct. In the process we have suggested that the opposite is actually the case and that the civilization which the dead white men brought into existence has been a great liberator of peoples everywhere. This is particularly true of women, racial minorities, homosexuals, transsexuals and as well as everybody else.

But be that as it may, we would now like to honor the spirit of racial equality and look at the deeds of dead males of other races. Let us begin today with *dead black males*□ and see what kind of works they have wrought. We are sure that few would disagree that after the long years of neglect they should be given their chance to shine.

Let us, then, inquire into the kind of civilization those guys have brought into being. What type of culture and socio-economic system they left behind as inheritance for future generations? What manner of contributions have they made to the general well-being and advancement of mankind? How do their scientific, technological, literary, philosophical, artistic achievements compare with those of their dead white counterparts?

If truth be told, the achievements of dead black males are less than you may think. When early European explorers first arrived in Africa, they observed that the indigenous civilization seems to be at an early iron stage of development. The indigenous populations – ruled over by the iron hand of black males – lived under most difficult and primitive conditions. They apparently did not know how to make use of the wheel and had no written language. As far as science, technology, philosophy, literature and jurisprudence are concerned, nothing of note had been accomplished or even apparently attempted. The religion was animistic, magic and voodoo in nature, devoid of any underlying systems of scriptures or developed theology. In terms of architecture, dead black males built no great cathedrals, public buildings or monuments. Most of their building efforts seem to have been confined to the construction of mud huts and simple wooden structures.

But let us not dwell on the fact that those dead black males made no practical contribution to the general welfare and betterment of the human race and left behind virtually nothing of significance in any area of human endeavor. It is likely they had no time for distractions such as science or philosophy, since they must have been fully preoccupied with building their fair and just societies. Given the multiculturalist trumpeting of virtues of non-white cultures, how could anyone doubt that those enlightened dead black guys ran societies in which women, racial minorities, homosexuals, transsexuals and everyone else must have been treated with utmost respect, dignity and equality?

We do not have the time or space to examine their tender handling of all identity groups so we will just focus on one: women. Nevertheless, seeing the compassion with which they treated one vulnerable demographic should give us some idea about how well they also treated the others. Our focus on women will undoubtedly please Western feminists who unceasingly complain about the alleged male oppression, domination and discrimination within our civilization stream. Surely those white males responsible for the creation of Western civilization will blush with shame in their graves once they hear how their black peers treated their own women.

When 19th century explorers arrived in South Africa, they were startled by the rather peculiar way in which females were handled by the indigenous black culture. Here is an account of a sympathetic explorer. We have quoted this passage previously, but it is worth repeating in this context:

The females, and especially the young ones are kept

principally among the old men, who barter away their daughters, sisters or nieces, in exchange for wives for themselves or their sons. Wives are considered the absolute property of the husband, and can be given away, or exchanged, or lent, according to his caprice ... Female children are betrothed usually from early infancy ... little real affection consequently exists between husbands and wives, a young man values a wife principally for her services as a slave.[88]

Without putting too fine a point on this, the (now dead) black gentlemen were not very nice to their ladies. Rather they displayed the form of male dominance that could only be described as barbaric. Sadly, the notion that women were not more than chattel seems to have been deeply rooted in the black male psyche as evidenced by much of African history. The evidence of historical misogyny and contempt for the female sex lives to this day, for example, in the practice of female circumcision which is still performed in the parts of Africa that suffer from a strong influence of the indigenous culture.

Black males have obviously treated women inhumanly in the past and their heirs continue their ruthless ways to this day. Contrast this with the attitude of the dead white males who were more than willing to grant distinction to women. Even as the 18th century European explorers were shocked to see the slave-like status of women in Africa, women in Europe were allowed to achieve the highest levels of intellectual and cultural pre-eminence.

It was the dead white males who were the first ones – and the only ones – among males of all races to come up with the ground-breaking notion that women are not inferior and that they deserve the same rights and dignity as men. This thought has apparently never crossed the minds of the dead black males. Furthermore, the dead white males were able to translate their noble ideas into reality by creating a societal system that granted full rights to women. The dead black men, on the other hand, never even thought of making such an attempt. In fact, they have always resisted such efforts and their descendants do so to this day.

Consider this paradox: to the extent that any black woman today is guaranteed rights – be they human, civil, legal or political – it is wholly due to the enlightened thinking and labor of dead white men. There are only two ways in which black women – or women of any color – can enjoy equal rights with men. They are either fortunate enough to be living in a western democracy (created by dead white males) or they live in non-western society which has been reformed by the civilizing influence of Western men. Therefore, black women today should be especially grateful to dead white males. If it was up to dead black males, they would be still treated like chattel and slaves. But it is not only black women, but women of all colors – black, white, brown, yellow, red – who should feel deep appreciation. This is because the dead white men were the only males in history who thought them worthy of holding equal status and they worked hard to secure it for them.

How paradoxical, then, that western feminists keep complaining about dead white males. And even though those angry feminists have apparently not noticed what those dead white males have done for them, others certainly have. One such perceptive observer is Ibn Warraq, the Pakistan-raised author and activist who has devoted his life to the reformation and secularization of Islamic culture. This is what he wrote: "The West is attacked as uniquely oppressive even though it has gained unprecedented rights and freedoms for women, for gays and lesbians, and for individuals in general."[89]

Ibn Warraq is, of course, absolutely correct. May we suggest that those western women who feel so oppressed in our society go and live in cultures erected and run by men of any other color be it black, brown, yellow or red. They would certainly not be accorded the rights, respect and consideration they receive in societies whose foundations have been laid by dead white males. Their very ability to complain is made possible by laws, guarantees and protections instituted by those white men. Black men in traditional cultures would certainly not tolerate such complaining although in their case it would actually be justified and true. Dead black males especially would be quick to put a stop to criticisms of this kind. A black eye would be a lucky outcome for the complaining ladies.

If you think that the treatment of women by the dead black man was appalling wait until you learn how they treated racial and ethnic minorities and other vulnerable groups. Hint: they did not treat them any better than they did their women. Former Zambian President Robert Mugabe, for example, described homosexuality as "un-African" and "a white disease." But this a subject for another essay. One only wonders what those complaining Western feminists and assorted social justice warriors would have to say about that. But anyone who knows anything about history and life cannot but observe with relief, "Thank God for those dead white men. Where would we be without them?"

THE LEFT'S WAY: VIOLENCE, FRAUD AND INTIMIDATION

A disturbing incident took place in Wayne County, Michigan last week. What happened is most instructive, because it exposes the modus operandi of the Atropic left as it tries to take over and subvert our society. It is important that we learn from this event and take measures to prevent its recurrence, because if we don't we will lose this country.

In Wayne County two Republican members of the county's Board of Canvassers, Monica Palmer and William Hartmann, initially refused to certify the results of the obviously fraud-ridden 2020 presidential election. Wayne County, by the way, includes the city of Detroit which has been continuously controlled by corrupt Democrats since 1962. Not surprisingly, Detroit has been known to suffer from election irregularities for many years. In this election, among other issues, around 70 percent of Wayne County precincts were found to be "out of balance," which means that the number of ballots cast did not match the number of people who signed in to vote.

The refusal to certify this vote made the two honest officials an immediate target of intimidation and blackmail. Within minutes of their decision, death threats began pouring in. "The [death] threats have been made against myself, my daughter and my husband," Monica Palmer told Detroit Free Press.[90] The threats that Monica Palmer referred to in this statement were conveyed to her privately. But there was more to come publicly so that the whole world could see just how vicious the American political left is.

In the contentious public meeting that followed the standoff, Palmer and Hartmann were abused and bullied by a succession of brazen and shameless Democrat operatives. In that meeting, which was broadcast on Zoom, Democrats made statements that contained threats of potentially deadly violence against the two board members and their families.

One of the oafs who used this tactic was a man by the name of Abraham Aiyash. Aiyash is a hard left activist who had just been elected to the Michigan House of Representatives. He hails from Michigan's deeply blue District 4 where he received nearly 90 percent of the vote. Prior to his election he worked as a trainer of community organizers. This is how a former co-worker described Aiyash in a recent Twitter post:

> I've worked closely with @AbrahamAiyash with his time working with @MichiganUnited, his job was training the next generation of organizers. Michigan should be proud to have such a fighter and a progressive champion in the state house, I know I am proud to call him a friend.[91]

At the Wayne County election certification meeting, this "progressive champion" wasted little time to set the scene by accusing Monika Palmer of racism:

> You are standing here today telling folks that Black Detroit should not have their votes counted. And know the facts. You are certainly showing that you are a racist. You may say that you are not. You may claim that you are not. But let's be very clear. Your words today and your actions today made it clear that you are okay with silencing the votes of an eighty-percent African-American city.[92]

Having accused and convicted Palmer of racism – which is apparently the worst charge that a person, living or dead, can face these days – Aiyash made his move:

> And what that tells us is you Miss Monica Palmer from Grosse Pointe Woods, which has a history of racism, uh, deciding to enable and continue to perpetuate the racist history of this country.[93]

Notice how deliberately Aiyash announced Palmer's name and the area of her residence. This was completely unnecessary as those present at the meeting were already aware of these facts. To understand what this man did and why, we need to remember the context in which he made his statement.

In the last six months we have watched terror unleashed in this country under the guise of anti-racism by the left and its militant organs BLM and Antifa. Apart from the unprecedented destruction of property, the crazed leftists have assaulted, beaten and brutalized scores of people, allegedly because of racism. To designate someone a racist in a high-stakes election meeting is to set them up as a candidate for violent retribution. To declare publicly that someone is a racist who intends to disenfranchise the whole black population of Detroit makes that person a target for potentially deadly violence.

Abraham Aiyash, however, did not stop with Monika Palmer. He continued further: "And I want you to think about what that means to your kids – who probably go to [name of the school] – and when they see all their black classmates..."

The leftist wretch publicly named the school that Palmer's children attend and then invited their "black classmates" to bully and abuse them.

This is obvious intimidation and blackmail. What Aiyash essentially said was this: "Either you will go along with us and certify this fraudulent election, or you and your family will be targeted for violence at home and in school."

But the leftists were still not done. Aiyash was followed by one Ned Staebler, who serves as Vice-President for Economic Development at Wayne State University. Lest you have any doubt where he stands politically, his Twitter name reads: "Ned BLACK LIVES MATTER Staebler." The capitalization 'Black Lives Matter' is his own.

Like so many Democrats today, Staebler is an unhinged individual who espouses extreme views. This is what he wrote to Trump's supporters in December 2016, barely a month after Trump's first presidential victory: "If you support Trump you are OK with bigotry, misogyny, xenophobia and a foreign power undermining our democracy. Own it."

During the Wayne County canvassers meeting last week, Staebler launched a fiery rant that set up Palmer and Hartmann as sitting ducks for leftist vengeance. This is what he said:

> I just want to let you know that the Trump stink, the stain of racism that you, William Hartmann and Monica Palmer, have just covered yourself in is going to follow you throughout history. Your grandchildren are going to think of you like Bull Connor or George Wallace. Monica Palmer and William Hartmann will forever be known in south-eastern Michigan as two racists who did something so unprecedented that they disenfranchised hundreds of thousands of Black voters in the city of Detroit...[94]

Notice the number of times Staebler says their names in connection with the term *racist*. This is deliberate. He continued:

> Just know when you try to sleep tonight, that millions of people around the world now on Twitter know the name Monica Palmer and William Hartmann, as two people completely racist and without an understanding of what integrity means or a shred of human decency. The law is not on your side, history won't be on your side, your conscience will not be on your side, and lord knows when you go to meet your maker your soul is

going to be very, very warm.[95]

Note the code words Staebler uses to turn the two canvassers into targets for BLM and Antifa terror: "racist," "black voters," "disenfranchise." Also disturbing are the ominous references to "your maker" and to "your soul," which obviously refer to posthumous existence.

Now put yourself in the shoes of these two vilified individuals. Imagine you were having to decide whether or not to certify the vote in this situation. How would you feel if the left's ire was about to come down on you and your children? I venture to say that most people could not withstand this kind of pressure and intimidation. It is no surprise, therefore, that the two commissioners shifted their position and went along with the left's demands.

An article in the Detroit Metro Times reported their change of mind this way:

> All eyes were on Wayne County on Tuesday evening as the county's election board, deadlocked in an unprecedented partisan vote, initially declined to certify Detroit's election results — only to quickly reverse course after concerned citizens called them out during the meeting's public comment.[96]

The report is only partially correct. The two Republicans did, indeed, reverse their stance, but not because they were "called out." They reversed because they and their families would have been terrorized if they hadn't. Most of us would likely do the same if faced with this level of danger and intimidation.

Note: subsequent to their reversal, Palmer and Hartmann tried to rescind their vote to certify by affidavit. Whether they will be successful or what will happen to them remains to be seen.

Regardless of the final outcome in Michigan, what we have seen there is the essence of the hard left's approach. This is exactly the way they take over governments and countries. It is never done in an honest or transparent way, but through chicanery, blackmail and violence.

In the weeks ahead this scenario will unfold up and down the US. Wherever decisions regarding this election will have to be made, the left will threaten and intimidate officials on all levels: local, state and federal. Every public official in favor of a meaningful audit or recount will be immediately marked for intimidation and violence. Sadly, in the present environment this threat is all too real. It is likely that in most cases the targeted officials will cave. Given the circumstances it would be difficult to blame them.

In a few days some of the legal cases will start making their way to the Supreme Court. Tremendous pressure will be put on those members who may be inclined to rule in favor of electoral integrity. Just put yourself, for example, in the shoes of the newly appointed Amy Coney Barrett. Should she vote in left's disfavor, she and her family would immediately become the targets of a nationwide campaign of hatred. For a mother of seven children this would not be an easy situation to handle. Her house would be besieged, and the members of the Barrett family would face harassment – or worse – wherever they go.

If we do not want to fall under the rule of the Atropic totalitarians of the hard left, it is imperative to confound their tactic of getting their way through intimidation and violence. There are two lines along which this problem must be tackled simultaneously. First, those officials who will be making election-related rulings must be given meaningful guarantees of security for themselves, their families and their property. They must know that they will be provided with whatever protection is necessary to keep them and their own safe.

Second, our government must take a strong stand against all forms of harassment. People like Abraham Aiyash and Ned Staebler should be charged with intimidation and incitement of violence against public officials. They will no doubt claim that this was not their intention but given today's violent climate, they knew exactly what they were doing. They publicly painted

Monika Palmer and William Hartmann as two inveterate racists and disenfranchisers of black people and then doxed them. In our current milieu this kind of tarring makes people prey for the left's Brown Shirt organs of BLM and Antifa. Such intimidation should not be tolerated in the United States of America and those who attempt it should feel the iron fist of the law.

BLACK PRIVILEGE

I t has been said over and over that all the rioting, looting and destruction that has been inflicted upon America in the last six months is due to racism. We have been told repeatedly that America is an irredeemably racist society that discriminates against black people. "Systemic" and "structural" are the terms used to describe the nature of America's alleged oppressiveness.

The stream of unceasing allegations has been kept up – unsurprisingly – by the political left. One of the recent examples is Michelle Obama who said this of Donald Trump in her pre-election message to the American people: "[W]hat the president is doing is, once again, patently false. It's morally wrong and, yes, it is racist."

Like the rest of them, Michelle Obama is a flagrant liar. Donald Trump is not a racist and neither is this country. There is no systemic or structural racism in American society. Quite to the contrary, in America black people enjoy an array of rights and advantages that are unavailable to the rest of the American population and can only be described as Black Privilege. And this privilege is very efficacious indeed.

It is ironic that Michelle Obama should play the race card given that she and her husband benefitted so richly from their Black Privilege. To begin with, Barack Obama – a black man – was elected to the highest office in what is a majority white country. He was elected not only once, but twice – in 2008 and again in 2012. The plurality of the votes that catapulted him to the presidency were cast by white people. The repeated election of a black man to the most prestigious post in American society should blow out of the water any claims of anti-black racism.

But this is not all. The reason why Barack Obama was elected was primarily because of the color of his skin. It would not be unfair to say that Mr. Obama was probably the most under-accomplished candidate to ever become a US President. A junior first-term senator from Illinois, his qualifications for the presidency were virtually nonexistent. By his own admission, his most consequential employment prior to his entry into politics was as a community organizer. As a senator, both on the state and federal level, he had little to show for it. He apparently neither sponsored nor originated any significant laws or initiatives. While a state senator he merely voted "present" on a number of occasions. Apparently being an agitator in the south side of Chicago and a good talker were his major qualification for office.

Such was Obama's background when he declared his candidacy for the highest office in this land. Were Mr. Obama white, he would have never gotten anywhere close to the Oval Office. Given his obvious lack of experience, a white Obama would have been laughed at the moment he announced his intention to seek the presidency. There can be no question that Obama was elected primarily because he is black. How could – we have to ask – such a thing happen in an allegedly racist country?

If Joe Biden should come out on top in this election, there is a great likelihood – given his enfeebled state – that within two years Kamala Harris would succeed him as president. Should this happen, it would mean that America would have two black presidents within six years. Both would be "affirmative action" presidents, since Kamala Harris was also chosen to be Biden's running mate primarily because she is black (the second reason was that she is a hard-left woman). Harris was certainly not selected because she is particularly competent or distinguished. In fact, her main talent seems to be bestowing sexual favors upon her political benefactors.[97] But such is the great power of Black Privilege that black men and women can be propelled into the

Oval Office despite their lack of accomplishments and qualifications.

Black Privilege, however, is not operative only in politics, but in every area of American society. In school admissions, for example, black candidates are blatantly advantaged over candidates of other skin colors, most notably whites and Asians. A couple of months ago, the US Department of Justice found Yale University to be in violation of federal anti-discrimination laws. Apparently at Yale black candidates were ninety percent more likely to be admitted than their white counterparts with roughly comparable credentials. This is nothing but blatant anti-white racism. Yale, of course, is not alone in this. This approach has been adopted in all spheres of American life: standards have been lowered for black people across the board in order to give them advantage over other racial groups.

Nor need we mention pro-black racism in government employment and contracting. Numerous welfare programs operate on an implicitly race-qualification basis, having been designed and tweaked to channel funds especially to blacks. Because of Black Privilege, black criminals receive special consideration in encounters with the police. Despite of what we have been told by leftist demagogues, black felons are treated more leniently than other racial groups. Indeed, black suspects are far less likely to be shot by the police than white suspects. This is not surprising, given the fact that that the use of force against blacks is treated with special severity by review boards and judicial bodies. And this holds true despite that fact that though blacks constitute only 13% of the population, they commit more than 50% of all violent crimes and murders. The truth is that most violent criminals and troublemakers in American society are black. By lowering the standards of acceptable behavior for blacks and by treating them with undue leniency, American society further encourages black criminality and delinquency... to everyone's harm.

The demagogues use misleading videos such as the one of George Floyd to assert that black people are routinely harassed and killed by the police. Such claims are simply preposterous. In 2019, fourteen unarmed black men were shot dead in the US by police.[98] Almost all of them posed imminent danger to others at the time they were killed. By way of contrast, several thousand black people were killed by other black people in the same period. The talk of black genocide by the police is just another of the left's monstrous lies. (By the way, George Floyd was not killed by his arresting cop. He died of a fentanyl overdose.[99])

We got to see Black Privilege up close during the recent and ongoing riots. We saw the videos of thousands of black youths rampaging, stealing and looting stores and businesses while the police just stood by, watching. Most of these criminals will never be brought to justice. They have been able to commit these crimes and get away purely because they are black. If white thugs ever attempted to loot and rampage in this fashion, they would be quickly dealt with by law enforcement. They would be shot on sight, as is customarily done in such situations. But the police would never do such a thing to black hoodlums. Such is the power of Black Privilege.

In America black people are being constantly excused and taken off the hook just because they are black. The truth is that there are two standards in this country: one is for blacks who are given preferential treatment and all kinds of advantages, and the other is for everyone else. Blacks get away with things that members of other races never would get away with.

How astonishing, then, that Michelle Obama would complain of racism. With a net worth of over 100 million dollars, the Obamas are richer than 99.9 percent of white people in America. And how did the Obamas amass their immense wealth and power? They have gained it through Black Privilege. And yet despite all of this, Michelle Obama said the following in her pre-election missive:

> I want everyone who is still undecided to think about all those folks like me and my ancestors, the millions of folks who look like me and fought and died and toiled as

slaves and soldiers and laborers to help build this country.

Yes, Mrs. Obama, we do think of you when we contemplate the racial situation in this country. What we see, however, is no lowly black slave but a wealthy and powerful woman who has obtained her great fortune on the back of her Black Privilege. If you and your husband were white, you would be just another suburban couple. It is because you are black that you were able to attain to the great heights of power and financial success. You can be sure most people do not like it when a person like you plays the race card in this manner. Frankly, you look phony when you speak like this.

What a wasted opportunity. A woman like Michelle Obama could have been a true leader for the black community. She could have been an example to those who look up to her – an example of gratitude to the country which provided such ample opportunities for its black citizens. Instead, she talks of slaves. Has she not noticed that we have long moved beyond that? After all, slaves are not elected president.

Here is truth to power for you: never in history has any minority had it as good as blacks have it in America today. The accusations of discrimination are an egregious lie. Our society has been set aflame on the basis of a complete fiction. Blacks today are rioting and complaining not because they have been discriminated against, but because American society has not been willing to enforce the basic standards of decency, morality and good behavior in the black community. Writing about the prevailing attitude of whites toward blacks, the great late black writer Walter Williams makes the same point: "Often, they accept behavior and standards from black people that they would not begin to accept from white people."[100]

In other words, what we are witnessing is a moral tragedy, not a racist one. This, however, is not the fault of black people. This situation has been deliberately created by white leftists. Sucked into the Atropic enterprise, the reason for their malevolence is the desire to subvert American society. More than six decades ago, they figured out that they could tear America apart by fomenting racial division and conflict. This they accomplished by destroying the moral fiber of the black community through such insidious mechanisms as the lowering of standards, undue leniency, over-indulgence and fostered dependency on the state. Once you ruin a racial demographic, there will inevitably follow anger, resentment and strife. We are now seeing the results of this subversion.

HITLER AND THE DEMOCRATS: LEFTWING KINDRED

"Michigan Democratic Rep. Brenda Lawrence compared President Donald Trump's presidency to Adolf Hitler's rule during the Holocaust" reported the outlet Just the News on September 2.[101] Please note that this statement was made in a public forum by a national level Democrat who is a member of the US House of Representatives.

Early in August Jim Clyburn, the House majority whip and one of the most powerful Democrats in Washington said this of Donald Trump on CNN: "I feel very strongly that he is Mussolini, Putin is Hitler."[102] Given how unhinged the Democrats are these days, we actually have to commend Clyburn for his relative restraint. The South Carolina democrat assigned Hitler status to Putin while being content to downgrade Trump to the level of the Führer's Italian sidekick.

Needless to say, the pejorative "Hitler" is the Left's favorite term of abuse which they hurl freely at those who disagree with them. But who really was Adolf Hitler? Since his name features so prominently in the left's language, it is important that we understand where he stood ideologically. Being clear about who Hitler was will be of great value. For one thing, this knowledge will help us identify those elements in our own political landscape that are ideologically allied with him. This, in turn, will enable us to protect ourselves against these elements and also give us the moral clarity to warn them of the dangerous path they are on.

When trying to come to grips with Hitler, we need to realize that he was first and foremost a socialist. Socialists, of course, come in different stripes and varieties. What they all invariably share, however, is their conviction that society should be commanded by the State. To put it another way, socialists hold the view that the State should be in charge. They think that the State should set the course not only for the nation's economy but also be in control of the public square as well as of the private lives of its citizens.

As a socialist – from the moment he seized power – Hitler was keen to build a strong centralized state that would control nearly every aspect of German life. Revealingly, the full name of his political party – which was the National Socialist Party also known as the Nazi Party – was "Nationalsozialistische Deutsche Arbeiterpartei." It translates into English as the *National Socialist German Workers' Party*. Notice the terms "Socialist" and "Workers" in the name. They immediately betray the nature of this organization: a typical socialist outfit. About this there can be little doubt. After all, why would the Nazis call themselves *socialists* if they did not believe themselves to be such?

Reviewing historical evidence in his essay titled "Hitler and the Socialist Dream," the renowned Cambridge scholar George Watson wrote:

> It is now clear beyond all reasonable doubt that Hitler and his associates believed they were socialists, and that others, including democratic socialists, thought so too. The title of National Socialism was not hypocritical.[103]

Would you like to know where Hitler got his socialism from? Writes Watson:

> Hitler acknowledged his profound debt to the Marxian tradition. "I have learned a great deal from Marxism" he once remarked, "as I do not hesitate to admit."[104]

So, Adolf Hitler was socialist who imbibed his leftist ways from none other than Karl Marx himself.

This brings us to a crucial point that will have far reaching consequences for our understanding of who Hitler was. As a socialist, Hitler is a leftist and therefore belongs on the left side of the political spectrum. Today it is generally believed that Hitler resided on the extreme right, but this is not the case. This untruth has been planted and spread by Western leftists who are for obvious reasons anxious to disown their notorious compadre. What gave the leftists a cover for their obfuscation was Hitler's racism and nationalism which he superimposed on his socialist underpinnings. This muddied the waters just enough to make the lie possible. The truth, however, remains that fundamentally Hitler was your standard socialist, somewhat downstream from total statists like Lenin, Stalin or Castro.

There is a saying that if something looks like a duck, quacks like a duck and walks like a duck, then it is a duck. We should apply the same principle here: If Hitler says that he is a socialist, has learned from a socialist, calls himself a socialist and quacks like a socialist, then he is a socialist.

Furnished with this knowledge, we can now place Hitler in his proper place on the political spectrum and see how he relates to other political actors of both past and present. Below is the political spectrum drawn correctly. Its basis is the prominence assigned by various players to the State vis-à-vis means of production, which is generally the most telling measure by which to evaluate their ideological position.

Political spectrum correctly drawn

We can now see that even though American Leftists continually accuse their opponents of being Hitler, it is actually themselves who qualify for this designation. Both being essentially socialist in orientation, Hitler's views on the role of the State place him roughly in the same region of the continuum as the bulk of the Democrat Party. This may come as a surprise to some people, but it is true nonetheless. Think of Bernie Sanders, for example, a self-confessed socialist from Vermont. Sanders, the most exciting Democrat politician today, enjoys a wide and enthusiastic support among the base.

Like those of "Nationalsozialistische Deutsche Arbeiterpartei," Sander's instincts and convictions are vibrantly socialist. The Washington Examiner notes:

> Vermont Sen. Bernie Sanders warmly praised Cuba and the Soviet Union in the late 1980s after visiting each, dismissing "horrors" in Cuba as right-wing propaganda and praising Soviet infrastructure even as dictatorship prevailed and the country was on the verge of collapse.[105]

Even the leftwing USA Today had to concede that Sanders "has made a lifelong career of ingratiating himself with anti-American radicals of various left-wing stripes."[106] We also learn that "Cuba's Marxist-Leninist revolution has been another one of Sanders' pet causes. In 1989, he issued a public statement piling praise on Castro's regime."

And this is what Bernie Sanders himself has said about that economic and social disaster known as the Republic of Cuba:

> For better or for worse, the Cuban revolution is a very profound and very deep revolution. Much deeper than I had understood. More interesting than their providing their people with free health care, free education, free housing ... is that they are in fact creating a very different value system than the one we are familiar with.[107]

Apart from the fact that Cuban hospitals are vermin-infested hell-holes and most Cubans live in shacks, Bernie is right on the money.

Here is an account of one of the latest victims of Cuban Healthcare who was put in a hospital as a result of having acquired COVID-19:

> We are in a terrible hospital, in awful sanitary conditions, when they give us food, they ask us to drink the soup from the plate, [without a spoon], there is not even toilet paper... they do not give us news of any kind, and it is impossible to talk with any doctor.[108]

But never mind this — Bernie still thinks Cuban Healthcare is excellent. It is informed views such as these that have made the socialist Sanders the most appealing and admired politician in the Democratic field today. So much so that Sanders would have won the 2016 Democratic presidential nomination if not for the machinations of the Clintonites at the Democratic National Committee who essentially stole it from him. If a socialist is the most popular politician in the Democratic party what does it tell you about the nature of this party? As for their views on the role of government vis-à-vis means of production, Sanders' followers would see eye to eye with Hitler's National Socialists. Ideological kin that they are, the two stand shoulder to shoulder on the left side of the political spectrum.

As radical as Sanders is, there are many prominent Democrats whose views place them even further to the left than Sanders. We can mention Alexandria Ocasio-Cortez, Ilhan Abdullahi Omar or Maxine Waters. If ever implemented, Ocasio-Cortez's New Green Deal would effectually require a complete takeover of the American economy by the State. Or take the Somali born hijab-clad Congresswoman Ilhan Omar who recently called for a complete dismantling of American society as we know it:

> We can't stop at criminal justice reform or policing reform. We are not merely fighting to tear down the systems of oppression in the criminal justice system. We are fighting to tear down systems of oppression that

exist in housing, in education, in health care, in employment, [and] in the air we breathe.[109]

The present system would be presumably replaced by some version of an all-powerful State which would eliminate all injustice
and guarantee perfect equity. Only such a State would have the
ability to fight the "oppression" that apparently exists even in
the air we inhale. Even Adolf Hitler himself would not call for
such far-reaching governmental powers. Clearly, the avowedly
socialist Hitler was more moderate in his views of the role of
the State than these American radicals. Some people may think
the comparison is unwarranted since these Democrats have not
wrought the kind of damage the Führer did. The difference,
however, is not in the extremity of their views but in the ability
to implement them. As of now, these Democrats have not had
the power or means to execute their radical agenda. Should they
succeed the results would undoubtedly be similar.

There are, in fact, striking affinities between today's hard
left and Hitler. When it comes to fundamentals such their
shared aversion to freedom of speech, silencing opposition,
cancel culture, political correctness, censorship, intimidation of
opponents, collectivism, etc. their positions and instincts are
practically indistinguishable. We have summarized these cor-
respondences in a graphic called *The Ideological Pedigree Table
of Values and Views*. It shows that today's hard left – which has
recently completed its capture of the Democrat Party – and au-
thoritarians like Hitler hail from the same psychological and
ideological root. Both are essentially leftwing totalitarians.

It could be said that the Democratic left is a present-day version of Hitler's National Socialists. The two could not be closer
as far as the first principles are concerned. Consider these parallels. Both Hitler and today's Left are decidedly socialist. They are
both intensely racist and use race as a central element of their
platform. Hitler's racism was primarily directed against Jews.
His form of racism is called antisemitism. Democrats' racism is
primarily directed against white people. We can call this form of

racism anti-whiteism. And for both the concept of their nation is of great importance albeit they spin it in reverse direction.

Democrats' Racism

If you should think that comparing the Democrats' racism to that of Hitler is an exaggeration, you only need to go to the riots which are now taking place all across America. These events are in reality nothing other than Democrat rallies organized and attended exclusively by the Democrat base none of whom would ever think of voting Republican. In fact, Trump voters are decidedly not welcome. If one gets ever identified as such, he or she is in immediate danger of grievous bodily harm or death. Only recently a Trump voter was murdered in cold blood during one such rally. His name was Aaron J. Danielson, and he was shot point black in the chest. When the news of his murder was announced, the assembled Democrats clapped and cheered in delight. Here is an account of their appalling celebration from the Portland Courant:

> A group rallying after the fatal shooting of Aaron J. Danielson celebrated the man's death. "We can take of the problem on our own. I am not sad that a f-cking fascist died tonight," an unknown woman yelled into a bullhorn. Cheers erupted from the crowd around her punctuated by people saying "yes!"[110]

As many have noticed, these Democrat convocations seethe with racism in which participants carry placards with inscriptions such as "F-ck Whiteness" while slogans such as "F-ck White People!" serve as their marching chants.

This is the Democratic base showing their true racist colors and the Democrat leaders and politicians not only refuse to condemn their racism, they openly and enthusiastically encourage the events where it takes place. What these mobs of Democrats are expressing in their chants and banners is the spirit and the soul of their party. Even Hitler and his mobs were not so public and brazen about their racism, and certainly not before they seized power.

Democrats' Negative Nationalism: Anti-Americanism

As we would expect from Hitler's ideological kin, the concept of their nation also plays a central role in Democrats' agenda. But while Hitler's nationalism was positive in orientation – he extolled the German Fatherland and culture – the Democrats' nationalism is negative: they denigrate their own country and their culture. The name of Hitler's positive nationalism was Deutscher Nationalismus. The name of the Democrats' negative nationalism is anti-Americanism.

The Democrats' anti-Americanism is on public display at their rallies in which the burning of the American Flag has become something of a regular ritual. And so are the chants "F-ck America." But it is not only the mobs of rank-and-file Democrat voters who harbor such views toward their nation. The dislike of America is shared by Democrats through all walks of life. To see that this is indeed so, you only need to ask yourself when was the last time you heard a Democrat say anything nice about their country.

Whenever they open their mouths on the subject of America, it is usually to denigrate and put her down. They regularly assert or imply that America is uniquely unjust and oppressive. They routinely claim that theirs is a country based on exploitation, slavery and oppression. From their tone you can sense that they think there is little good about America or her past. When the President of the United States was giving his 4th of July speech this year under the Mount Rushmore, a well-known moderator for a major TV network said that the talk was being given on the land stolen from the Indians under statues of slave owners. Both claims were specious, but this just shows you what American leftists truly think of their own country: they can never find anything good in it. The fact that America has created the most affluent society in history where all people enjoy equal rights and full freedoms somehow escapes their notice. What they also do not notice is the fact that America has for the better part of the past century been the most desirable place to be.

People from all over the world have been eager to immigrate to America, because in their view it was the best society on the planet to live in. And they were probably right. This, however, is quickly changing now as the Democrats – which are now virtually indistinguishable from the Hard Left – are doing their best to destroy American society, its institutions and its values. In the last four months alone, the Democrat mobs have managed to burn dozens of American cities. These violent rioters are nothing other than the equivalent of Hitler's notorious brownshirts.

Being Hitler's kindred and, like him, driven by Atropos' anti-western animus, it is no surprise that Democrats' works result destruction. As Hitler ruined Germany, so will Democrats ruin America if they ever manage to gain power. It should be the hope of all good and patriotic American that this never happens. As a warning and as instruction to those who still do not see the Democrats' real nature, we present a table of similarities between these two destructive, racist and anti-humane organizations.

	HITLER/NAZIS	DEMOCRATS
The role of the State	Control of society and individual	Control of society and individual
Position on the ideological spectrum	Socialist	Socialist
Race politics	Intense racism	Intense racism
Type of racism	Anti-Semitism	Anti-Whiteism
Racist practice	"Burn Jews"	"F-ck Whites"
Nationalism	Yes	Yes
Direction of nationalism	Positive	Negative
Type of nationalism	German - Nationalism	Anti-Americanism

As you can see, both the Democrats' and Hitler's programs revolve around the same three basic planks:

- Socialism
- Racism
- Nationalism

The minor variations between them – such as the target of racism and the positive/negative orientation of nationalism – are merely due to the somewhat different circumstances and times in which these totalitarians operate.

To express it another way, change Hitler's target of racism from Jews to whites and his German nationalism to anti Americanism and what you get are today's Democrats. Revealingly, the two agree on nearly everything from their violent tactics down to their shared dislike of America.

We would do well to contemplate the implications of this carefully.

ATROPIC KIN: THE PROGRESSIVE LEFT HOLDS THE SAME VALUES AS TYRANTS AND OPPRESSORS OF THE PAST

One the most frequently used debate tactics of today's Left is comparing their opponents to tyrants who ruled in opposition to the western tradition of openness and freedom. The names such as "Hitler," "Stalin" and "Mao" are regularly hurled by the Woke against whoever opposes them, which usually happen to be people who hold some variety of conservative or traditional beliefs. Levelling pejoratives at their interlocutors is, in fact, the progressive left's principal and most favored form of argument whenever their views are questioned.

By now we are all too familiar with the following scenario which keeps repeating itself with monotonous predictability: A progressive makes a claim about our society or the nature of relations within it. An opponent counters this contention by presenting evidence to the contrary. Instead of engaging with the evidence, the social warrior becomes angry and claims to be offended. He or she then begin begins to shout and accusations of "Hitler," "fascist" and such fly in a quick succession.

But are such accusations really justified? Do conservatives have the same mindset or hail from the same ideological pedigree as Hitler, Stalin or Mao? And what about those who so self-righteously level these accusations? Where do they really stand in all of this? What are their own ideological roots and credentials?

Fortunately, there is a relatively easy way to cut through the froth of passions and heated rhetoric to get at the truth of the matter. We will do this by taking the three classes in question – tyrants, progressives and conservatives – and place them side by side. We will then look at how their values compare in regard to important issues of practical politics and philosophy. This should help clarify the situation by bringing out the underlying political pedigrees and ideological links.

For the purposes of illustration and personal relatability, we will choose typical representatives for each class. For the first two groups the choices are easy and obvious. Thus, the tyrant category will be represented by the usual suspects: Hitler, Stalin, Mao, Pol Pot, Castro and Kim Jong-un. Those in the leftist column will be broadly represented by those who in the contemporary political parlance are called the Woke. The Woke encompass large swathes of today's Left and include those who would call themselves progressives and social justice activists which, in turn, span subgroups such as anti-racist activists, feminists, BLM, the militant LGBT, homosexual and trans activists among others.

The choice of personnel on the conservative side is more difficult, since it is not easy to find a genuine specimen on the contemporary scene. Most of those who call themselves "conservative" today have compromised their principles in order to appease the media and their progressive critics. From our perspective, there are two well-known living political figures who broadly embody the principles of traditional conservatism. They are Ron Paul and Pat Buchanan. Their worldview is not identical since they each give different weight to different aspects of conservatism. Nevertheless, they are both unmistakable bearers of this tradition whose modern foundations have been laid by Adam Smith and Edmund Burke. Both Ron Paul and Pat Buchanan are former presidential candidates who have exerted considerable intellectual influence and attracted substantial following. However, their refusal to compromise their principles has alienated the Republican establishment and cost them the nomination. Needless to say, each is in his own way is a great moral force.

Even though Dr. Paul is usually called a libertarian in the larger historical context, he would be more aptly described as a classical liberal or a traditional conservative. The main reason he is labelled a libertarian today is to distinguish him from the faux conservatives who have muddled the waters of political discourse. These are people who are not conservatives in the true sense of the term, but who nevertheless managed to appropriate this name for themselves. Such types would comprise, for example, the assorted neo-conservatives and moderate leftists who, for reasons of political expediency, insist on being called "conservative." Some examples would include John Kasich, Mitt Romney, Jeff Flake, Chuck Hegel and William Kristol. Some of them have already signaled they will vote for Joe Biden in the upcoming election. Obviously, anyone voting for the leftist Biden-Harris ticket cannot be a real conservative. And even though these so-called conservatives are sometimes called "Hitlers" and "Stalins" by the progressives, it is only because they are less extreme than those who hurl such accusations.

We now turn to a comparison of positions, view and values held by the representatives of the three categories under examination. We present this information in a graphic which we call *"The Ideological Pedigree Table of Values and Views."*

The Ideological Pedigree Table of Values and Views

	Totalitarians / Tyrants (Hitler, Stalin, Mao, Pol Pot, Castro, Kim)	The Woke / Progressives / Social Justice Warriors (Race, Feminists, Homosexual, Trans Activists, BML, LGBT)	Traditional Conservatives/ Classical Liberals (Ron Paul, Pat Buchanan)
Tolerance of opposing views	No	No	Yes
Freedom of expression	No	No	Yes
Freedom of speech	No	No	Yes
Political Correctness	Yes	Yes	No
Cancel culture	Yes	Yes	No
Freedom of conscience	No	No	Yes
Free and truthful press	No	No	Yes
Repression of dissenting views	Yes	Yes	No
Demonization of objectors	Yes	Yes	No
Punishment of dissenters	Yes	Yes	No
Discrimination	Yes	Yes	No
Equal treatment	No	No	Yes
Equality before the law	No	No	Yes
Autonomy of the individual	No	No	Yes
Civil liberties	No	No	Yes
Respect for private property	No	No	Yes
Collectivism	Yes	Yes	No
Promise of Utopia	Yes	Yes	No

The first thing we notice is that except for the very last item there is a unanimous agreement on fundamental principles and values between today's progressives and social justice warriors on one hand and totalitarians on the other.

What this clearly shows is that the woke left espouses the same elemental attitudes as the tyrants of the past and present. As far as the basic questions of human life and governance go, their thinking is identical. The two classes share the same mind-set and inclinations. Psychologically and ideologically, they are cut from the same cloth.

Many people will be startled by this and may think that in putting together this information we have used some sleight of hand to make the progressive left look bad. Let us reassure you that this is not the case and that what you see is a straight-forward depiction of reality. The graphic above is nothing other than a simple statement of facts. What makes it striking is the way in which these facts are presented. Our approach cuts through political posturing, deception and demagoguery to the basic values that define the worldview of each class. It then organizes this information in a way that brings out the ideological affinities and fault lines, showing where different groups stand in relation to one another.

In a certain sense, the above matrix is to the study of political phenomena as the Periodic Table of Elements is to the study of chemical ones. Mendeleyev's Table cuts through the surface appearances – such color, odor, texture, etc. – to the underlying essentials. A perceptive man who would not let superficials mislead him, Mendeleyev focused on fundamental properties – the atomic number and electron configuration – and used their values to achieve a highly revealing classification of elements. He then displayed his results in a visually clear way that enables the student to grasp the truth of the matter quickly and intuitively. When we look at the Periodic Table, we can immediately see where various elements fit as well as where they stand in relation to one another. Those equipped with this knowledge can see things for what they are and not be fooled by appearances. To the uninitiated, gilding may seem like gold, but when a chemist ascertains the atomic number of the thing in his hand, he can easily distinguish the fake from the real.

As Mendeleyev's Periodic Table mapped out the realm of elements, the *Ideological Pedigree Table* seeks to map out the ideological landscape. When you encounter an ideological phenomenon – be it a movement, a teaching or a leader – by evaluating it against the values in the Table you will be able to see exactly what kind of *political* element they are. In the same way that a skilled chemist scientifically ascertains the intrinsic grossness of a metal though it may be covered in gilding, you will now be able to see through the progressives' veneer of compassion to recognize that they are actually totalitarians at heart.

Let us now make a few remarks and observations on the graphic above.

Based on the information it contains, we can plainly see that – ideologically and attitudinally – the progressives, the Woke and the tyrants are close kin. Even though their language may superficially differ depending on the time and place in which they operate, underneath the rhetoric there is a shared unity of underlying attitudes. Their goal is invariably the same: Atropic rejection of the traditional western principles of liberty and freedom in favor of totalitarian control over their fellow citizens. It could be said that these people belong to a shared brotherhood of oppression.

Because they know well that their positions are indefensible by reason, open discussion is anathema to both the woke and the tyrants. Freedom of speech and expression are their scourge, because their worldview cannot withstand the light of truth. This is why they all seek to suppress it by instituting various forms of political correctness.

Every totalitarian without exception advocates some form of political correctness. Political correctness is the favored instrument of totalitarians of all stripes with which they endeavor to silence their opponents. It prevents the articulation of facts that are plainly obvious but inconvenient to those who seek to seize or maintain political power by illicit and undemocratic means. In an environment ruled by political correctness truth must not be spoken. Instead, one must either stay silent or say the *opposite* of the truth.

Political correctness takes different forms depending on how much power the totalitarians possess in a given society. In democratic societies it takes the form of institutional speech codes. In totalitarian societies it takes the form of outright state censorship.

All totalitarians – from the mass-murdering tyrants to the

progressives and the woke – insist on a cancel culture. The cancel culture is the executory arm of political correctness. Its purpose is to punish those who cross the bounds of acceptable speech. The severity of cancellation methods depends on the degree of power that totalitarians wield. The more power they possess, the more severe the modes of cancellation. In our society modes of cancellation range from being removed from platforms of public discourse to being fired from one's job. In totalitarian societies, the cancellation modes normally range from imprisonment to death.

Firing is the highest and most favored mode of cancellation of both the progressives and the tyrants. In our society where progressive totalitarians do not yet possess full state power, serious offenders are cancelled by being *fired* from their jobs. In totalitarians societies serious offenders are cancelled by a *firing* squad.

Totalitarians living under democratic systems of government have to settle for less drastic methods of cancellation such as deletion of social media accounts and destruction of dissenters' reputation and livelihood. These forms of cancellation, however, are not foolproof. The cancelled can still open another account under a different name and continue propagating their subversive ideas about free speech, freedom of conscience, equal treatment and such.

When directed against dissenters, the bullet, the noose and the gas chamber are nothing other than the manifestations of the cancel culture. These methods are beloved by the tyrants, because they constitute the quickest and the most effective modes of cancellation. They guarantee that persons thus cancelled will never again engage in politically incorrect speech.

Some people may think that today's progressives and social justice warriors cannot be cut from quite the same cloth as Hitler and Stalin, since they are not guilty of the same depredations. The evidence presented above, however, clearly shows that they are indeed of the same heart and mind. The reason they have not committed the excesses of their Atropic kin is because they lack the power to do so. To accomplish what Hitler, Stalin and Mao have accomplished you must be in full control of the state apparatus. As of now, western progressives do not have that power, but they are doing their best to obtain it. Because they are actuated by identical beliefs, if they ever attain that power, they will undoubtedly use it in the same fashion their tyrannical brothers have used theirs.

All tyrants mentioned above have ruined their societies and left millions of corpses in their wake. The progressives will do the same if they ever attain unchecked state power. This is inescapable, since they subscribe to the same basic values and principles.

Most woke snowflakes are not some gentle caring beings they pretend to be. This is only a mask. This kind of deception and pretense is pervasive among leftists and has, in fact, been the left's modus operandi since the French Revolution. Underneath their posture of fragility, the snowflakes are ruthless hooligans who through various forms of activism and online thuggery have destroyed the reputations and lives of many good people. Cancel-happy, politically correct, intolerant in their attitudes and merciless when dealing with dissenters, today's snowflakes are the scions of tyrants.

Despite being regularly accused of being so, true conservatives are certainly no Hitlers or Stalins. Quite to the contrary, conservatives hold positions, views and values that are in direct oppositions of those jointly espoused by progressives and tyrants.

The pejoratives that the woke hurl at conservatives are completely ungrounded. Unlike progressives, conservatives share no attitudes or principles with the likes of Stalin, Hitler or Mao. The accusations the progressives make against conservatives are a form of self-projection. The condemnations they direct at their opponents actually apply to themselves.

The progressive-social-justice Left encounters little political opposition these days, because the so-called conservatives have sold out their principles and lack the moral fiber to stand up to the left's Atropic, inhumane, anti-Western agenda of oppression and destruction.

The values and principles that the progressive left and tyrants jointly espouse are illiberal, anti-Western and dangerous. If implemented, they cannot but result in despotism, destruction and murder on a large scale. This is the clear lesson and warning of history. Well-meaning, good people should be aware of this. They should not be fooled by the left's disingenuous rhetoric and false posturing but should look carefully at what these people really believe and stand for. Forces of oppression and tyranny always initially present themselves as angels of light and liberation. Once in power, however, their true nature manifests itself with tragic consequences. By then, however, it is usually too late to reverse the course.

There is much more to be said about this, and we shall continue shortly. In the meantime, let us contemplate *The Ideological Pedigree Table of Values and Views* with care so that we can fully digest the information it contains. It lays bare an important truth about the Atropic forces that are currently attempting to subvert and take over our society.

THE POLITICAL SPECTRUM: THE CORRECT DELINEATION

I f we want to navigate through complex territory, we need an accurate map. If we do not have a good map, we are likely to get lost. If we want to understand the political landscape, we need a sound paradigm by which to orientate ourselves. If we do not have a good paradigm, we are likely to lose our bearing and make wrong judgments. One of the reasons why so much of our political discourse is so confounding and unfruitful is because our paradigm is faulty.

The left-right map we have been given to navigate the political landscape is incorrect. It depicts the political spectrum as popu-lated on the far left by hardline communists and socialists such as Lenin, Stalin, Castro. On the other end – on the far right – we have fascists like Hitler and Mussolini. These two camps stand on the opposite extremes and in between there is everyone else. In this model, the American Democrats are left of center while the Republicans are right of center.

Incorrect: Conventional understanding of the political spectrum

```
Stalin        Dems          GOP        Hitler
|----------------|------center------|------------------|
LEFT                                      RIGHT
```

Here is how you can quickly see there something wrong with this paradigm: both Stalin and Hitler were socialists and big government totalitarians whose ideological underpinnings had their roots in the teachings of Karl Marx (see here[111]about Hitler's socialism). But if these two delineate the whole length of the political spectrum, where, then, do we fit limited government types such classical liberals or today's libertarians? In the conventional understanding, there is really no place for them.

Below is the political spectrum drawn in a way that encompasses the full width of the political landscape.

Correct delineation of the political spectrum

```
Total State                    Minimal State
|-----------------center----------------|
LEFT                               RIGHT
```

In this paradigm, the spectrum is delineated by the degree of statism *intended* and *aspired* to by various political actors and ideologies. Thus, on the extreme left you have statist totalitarians while on the opposite side you have non-statists and state minimalists.

Actors on the political spectrum

With the corrected paradigm, we now easily find a proper place for classical liberals and libertarians. At the same time, Hitler – a Nazi socialist who built a powerful German state – is placed where he belongs on the left side, somewhat downstream from full-out statists like Stalin, Lenin or Castro.

Some observations on the correctly delineated spectrum

We now see that the conventional paradigm only presents the left portion of the spectrum and not the whole extent of it.

This misunderstanding has been consciously planted and cultivated by the left which had several good reasons for propagating this distortion. Their first concern was to distance themselves from Hitler, their socialist brother. We explained elsewhere how they were able to pull it off: "What gave the leftists a cover for their obfuscation was Hitler's racism and nationalism which he superimposed on his socialist underpinnings. This muddied the waters just enough to make the lie possible. The truth, however, remains that fundamentally Hitler was your standard socialist."

The obfuscation enabled leftists appear to be removed from or even opposite of Hitler. This was a masterstroke of propaganda given that Hitler is their ideological bedfellow. We have shown previously how the two share fundamental inclinations in the Ideological Pedigree Table of Values and Views. As such, they stand shoulder to shoulder on the political spectrum. Hitler was a leader whose socialism was mixed with strong elements of racism and nationalism. Today's Democratic party – which has been recently taken over by its radical elements – is a present-day version of the Nazis in the American context. Both are socialists who are strongly racist and nationalistic. The only difference is the target of their racism – whites vs Jews – and the direction of their nationalism: negative vs positive.

The left's inversion of the political paradigm has had the further advantage of placing their ideological opponents – those advocating a more limited state – on the same half of the spectrum as Hitler thus creating an appearance of affinity even though in reality they are opposites.

By placing themselves close to the center, leftists have managed to make themselves look moderate and reasonable. Their feigned ideological modesty was designed to increase their appeal to the common man for whom they purport to care. Nothing, however, could be further from the truth. The moment leftists gain power they make life miserable for the very people they claim to champion. Just ask the workers of the Soviet Union, Hitler's German Volk, Mao's peasants or the people of Cuba how good and pleasant was life under their leftist rulers.

On the most fundamental level, a leftist is someone who advocates state control over the means of production. This control can be complete or partial. It can be in the form of direct ownership by the state or by indirect ownership through state-mandated entities or agents. Control over the means of production can also be achieved through various forms of legislative, administrative and regulatory mechanisms. The degree of control *intended* determines where on the left side of the spectrum one stands.

The left side of the political spectrum can be broadly divided into two parts: the hard left and the soft left. The line of demarcation is not always sharply defined. Hard leftists advocate complete or near-complete socialization of the economy and a powerful centralized state. Thus, their agenda is Atropic in nature as it runs in direct opposition to the evolution of Western political tradition. Moderate or soft leftists advocate a less statist arrangement. The hard left is always made up of either actual or potential totalitarians and murderers. To the soft left belong, for the most part, the self-serving bunglers.

Division of the political left into two zones

It is impossible to exercise a significant measure of control over the means of production without becoming authoritarian. This is because such control goes against the natural flow of things. To achieve it, you need coercion and violence (or at least the explicit threat of it). The greater the degree of control you seek, the more authoritarian you must become. Complete or near complete control requires one to become a totalitarian. Such a high level of state control over the means of production can only be implemented through mass murder. This has been the case in every country where such control has been achieved (see The Black Book of Communism[112]). It is a kind of Faustian bargain:

you gain power and control but in return you have to sell your soul, i.e., you must oppress, coerce and kill. Apparently, certain types do it quite gladly.

Socialists are leftists. The terms socialist and leftist can be used interchangeably although only in a rough and imprecise way. There have been many different modes and varieties of socialism – both attempted in practice and formulated as theories – and this term is very difficult to define. Even socialists themselves do not agree on what socialism actually means or entails and there are constant arguments and infighting among them. Given the lack of definitional clarity in regard to the term *socialism*, it is generally more productive to use the term leftist instead.

On the hard left you have traditional communists and far left socialists including the Nazis. On the soft left you would have the post-war western European socialist and labor parties. Today's GOP and the Conservative Party in Great Britain also belong to the right side of the soft left. Political parties are not permanently fixed at one position on the spectrum; they tend to move and shift within a certain range depending on which faction controls them at any given time. We have seen an instance of a fairly dramatic move recently in the US where the Democratic Party has been taken over by the extreme elements within its ranks and consequently lurched sharply leftward. As it currently stands, the US Democratic Party is a hard left party controlled by left-wing radicals and it behaves accordingly. For example, its highest officials openly encourage rioting, violence and destruction of cities while deliberately tying the hands of law enforcement and shielding perpetrators from prosecution. The latest instance of this is the Democratic vice-presidential candidate Kamala Harris who recently praised Black Lives Matter as "brilliant."[113]

As you may know, BLM is a violent revolutionary outfit founded by Marxists.[114] The riots that have torn America apart and caused billions of dollars in damage have been conducted under the auspices of BLM, which has launched this destructive movement under the false pretenses of systemic racism. Senator Harris's praise of BLM comes on the heels of her June interview in which she openly called on BLM and their collaborators to continue the violence and destruction.[115] This is what she said:

> Everyone beware because they're not gonna stop. They're not gonna stop before election day in November, and they're not going to stop after election day. And everyone should take note of that... they're not going to let up—and they should not. And we should not.

Please note that this statement was not made by some fringe anarchist. This incitement to lawlessness, violence and anarchy is coming from the highest echelons of the Democratic party. Also please notice Harris' use of the pronoun "we" in the last sentence. This is an explicit acknowledgement that Democrats on the highest levels approve of and are part of this violent criminal movement.

Not to be outdone, and in keeping with the tried-and-true tactics of the hard left, Hillary Clinton, former Democratic nominee for president, has called on Democrats – in direct subversion of the democratic process – not to concede the upcoming election "under any circumstances." This is how she put it: "Joe Biden should not concede under any circumstances, because I think this is gonna drag out and eventually I do believe he will win if we don't give an inch."[116]

Hillary Clinton's stance is indicative of the present dynamic within the Democratic party. Having begun as a leftist radical in the 60s, Clinton became in her ripe age a hardened establishment politician for whom considerations of power and money took precedence over her youthful socialist ideals. Her transformation was so complete that she eventually became something of a neocon. So much so that a number of high-level Republican operatives voted for her over Donald Trump in the 2016 elections.[117] But with the recent capture of her Party by its radical elements, Hillary Clinton – in an apparent effort to remain relevant internally – has moved sharply leftward, closer toward her youthful roots. As a proper radical, she now openly advocates the subversion of democracy and election theft. It would not be at all surprising if one of these days she goes all out and begins speaking of Revolution. This is truly a pity, because Mrs. Clinton has arrived at a point in her life where she could at least attempt to bring some sanity and moral sense into the bad situation. She could try to position herself the Grand Dame of the Democratic Party and condemn the criminal behavior of the democrat mobs who are ravaging and terrorizing this country. But rather than doing what is right and decent, she is pouring more vitriol on the fire.

Both Kamala Harris and Hillary Clinton know exactly what they are doing. With the left's ugly nature now on full display, they sense they are going to lose electorally, but this does not discourage them in any way. They will instead try to gain power by other means. After all, the hard left has rarely come into power via the democratic process. The reason for this is quite simple: people generally grasp that despite their rhetoric there is something deeply wrong with these leaders and their twisted programs. As a result, socialists and communists almost invariably seize power through undemocratic means such as coup d'états, insurrections, parliamentary coups, election theft and such. These high-level Democratic politicians behave exactly like the Nazi and Bolshevik operatives did in their time. In a repeat of history, their gangs of looting followers on the streets of America are the equivalent of Hitler's Brown Shirts and Lenin's red mobs.

People who gravitate toward the hard left are usually driven there by the dark impulses of their psyches which they seek to discharge through political activism. This has been true in the past and it is also true now. Many of the far-left leaders have been narcissist psychopaths with little or no empathy for fellow human beings. These days you can observe the connection between psychological disturbance and far left activism when you watch the woke and progressives in action.

The vast majority of them are clearly troubled individuals. They are usually highly self-absorbed, angry and emotionally disturbed. You may have seen a viral video of a liberal woman having a meltdown over the death Ruth Bader Ginsburg while driving a car which recently made its rounds around the internet. This is what she shrieks in part:

> Holy f—king shit, you guys! I am driving the car but I just go a notification that Ruth Bader Ginsberg died! F-ck! Could this year get any f-cking worse?![118]

The woman then howls and shakes as if she were possessed. If you watch the video, you will notice that she is not actually upset about the death of a human being but about the fact that Ruth Bader Ginsburg did not manage to hang on a little longer so that Trump would be deprived of the opportunity to nominate her replacement before the election. "Ruth," she screams wildly, "you just had to make it to 2021!"

Needless to say, the woman looks better adjusted than most of her ideological compadres these days. Apart from the obvious lack of empathy, many among the woke also exhibit sexual abnormalities of various kinds such as homosexual behavior or thinking that they belong to the opposite biological sex (a condition known as gender dysphoria). Some woke activists even claim there are more than one hundred types of gender.[119] When the British TV show host Piers Morgan challenged this idea late last year the woke launched a campaign to have him cancelled. These days you can find these cancel types at the ongoing BLM riots where they shout and scream about a problem that does not exist.

Needless to say, these types are angry, intolerant, unloving and vindictive. They are ever ready to cancel and destroy anyone who disagrees or opposes them. They exhibit the same tendencies that the hard left has always displayed: hatred of free speech, proclivity toward violence, suppression of dissent, racism, atheism, dehumanization of opponents, accusations of thought crimes, intimidation of dissenters, etc. Should they obtain the power they so feverishly seek, they will undoubtedly use it in the same cruel ways their ideological brothers have always done.

RED ALERT: A REVOLUTION IN PROGRESS IN THE USA

In the last four months America has experienced violence and upheaval not seen since the Civil War. Widespread rioting and burning cities have been the order of the day. We have witnessed anarchy and destruction on an unprecedented scale. Our nation has been vilified and accused of being irredeemably racist. Ritual kneelings took place on all levels: from people in the streets to politicians in the highest echelons of our government. We have seen shameless pandering and the political class bitterly divided. We watched law enforcement standing by while the rioters looted and burned with impunity.

These events have caught most people by surprise. Especially startling has been the speed with which these developments have unfolded. A mere few months ago, we were an apparently well off and stable country. Today our nation seems to be falling apart at the seams and slouching toward a civil war. In February of this year, Gallup released a poll which showed that Americans' confidence in the U.S. economy was at a 20-year high.[120] At that time nearly ninety percent of Americans were happy with the course of their personal lives. Barely eight months later, we are a country on the verge of anarchy and lawlessness. How could it happen? Why did it happen? Most people just cannot make sense of this.

There is, however, a definite reason and explanation for the upheaval and disturbance in America today: what we are witnessing is a revolution in progress.

This may come as something of a shock to many, but it is sadly true. The forces that are attempting to carry out this revolution are, in fact, quite explicit about it. Those marching in the streets routinely chant revolutionary slogans and carry placards featuring the word "REVOLUTION." To make their purpose unmistakably clear, they regularly deface buildings with graffiti of sickle and hammer and other revolutionary symbols.

Below is a first-hand account of an event which took place as part of the so-called anti-racism "protests" in June of this year in New York City:

> With masses cheering the several calls for communist revolution, we marched down one of Brooklyn's busiest streets, Flatbush Avenue. Bus drivers blared their horns and raised their fists as we chanted the names of Black youth murdered by the racist police, while marching past graffitied and smashed-up NYPD police cars.[121]

This unfolding revolution has been launched by the Atropos-beholden hard left and its goal is to topple our society and replace it with an altogether different system of governance.

The underlying ideology that informs the thinking and actions of the revolutionaries is Marxism and its derivatives and modalities such critical race theory, Cultural Marxism, liberation theology and the like. The revolutionaries call themselves by different names such as Marxists, communists, socialists, progressives, liberals, Democrats and such. (Not all who describe themselves as Democrats and liberals are Marxists, but some are.)

At this time the revolution is being spearheaded by the organization known as Black Lives Matter (BLM). BLM is frank about its agenda and ultimate goal. The headline video on its website is called "Now, We Transform."[122] The teaser underneath reads: "Our fight for liberty, justice, and freedom continues. Together, we can — and will — transform. This is the revolution."

When these people call for a revolution, they do not mean some kind of partial change or reform. What they want is a complete remaking and transformation of the American system.

The founders of BLM are trained and committed Marxists. The New York Post reported the following fact this summer:

> Black Lives Matter co-founder Patrisse Cullors said in a newly surfaced video from 2015 that she and her fellow organizers are "trained Marxists" – making clear their movement's ideological foundation, according to a report. Cullors, 36, was the protégé of Eric Mann, former agitator of the Weather Underground domestic terror organization, and spent years absorbing the Marxist-Leninist ideology that shaped her worldview.[123]

Patrisse Cullors and other leaders of Black Lives Matter make no secret of their desire to overthrow American society. They may be closer to their goal than most people can imagine.

The BLM inspired terror and upheaval of the past four months has followed the pattern of Marxist revolution that has unfolded dozens of times in the past 100 years. It features the following components:

- Intense hatred of the existing order by the leaders of the revolutionary movement
- Demoralization of the population by propaganda, blame, intimidation and terror
- Delegitimization of law enforcement and existing governmental structures
- Destabilization of society by violence
- Inversion of moral values
- Subversion of law and order
- Generation of lawlessness and anarchy

The revolutionary movement has achieved a significant measure of success on all of these fronts, making our society ripe for being overthrown and taken over by the Marxist insurgents.

Some Observations

This revolutionary movement did not begin with the riots that erupted on May 26, 2020 in Minneapolis and spread like a wildfire across the United States. The groundwork had been laid decades before. Its roots can be traced to the 1960s, and its precursors go even further back.

This work has been carried out by individuals and groups harboring intense dislike of western values and intent upon seeing American society radically changed or overthrown. Almost all of them drew – in one way or another – their ideological nourishment and inspiration from the ideology of Marxism or its offshoots.

What the revolutionaries seek most of all at this particular point in their struggle is the breakdown of law and order, because this is the state of affairs whereby they can seize control. In some jurisdictions they have already succeeded. Our institutions are now starting to prosecute citizens who are trying to protect themselves and their communities against the depredations of the destructive Atropic mobs. We have seen this with Kyle Rittenhouse, Mark and Patricia McCloskey and others. Until recently, it was considered perfectly acceptable in this country to defend one's life and property against criminal predators. Today those who try to exercise this right are themselves treated as criminals while the actual criminals are allowed to roam free.

This constitutes a complete change of worldview, which makes us vulnerable to an overthrow. With the breakdown of law and order and with a demoralized population and paralyzed law enforcement, we are a country which is on the verge of being taken over by the hard left.

Because of the havoc the left has wrought, the unfolding revolution has a good chance of succeeding. When you study history, you learn that revolutions take place very quickly – usually in a matter of weeks – before most people have had a chance to realize what is happening. This is where we find ourselves today.

There is no question that this is an hour of great peril for America. What we face is nothing less than a national emergency. We must see, therefore, see the unfolding events for what they are and take appropriate measures to stem this immoral Marxist revolutionary movement. If the Marxists have their way, calamity and misery of unimaginable proportions will ensue, as they always do when revolutions of this kind succeed.

THIS IS A MARXIST REVOLUTION

I n our recent posts we have tried to show that the upheaval that is presently convulsing this country is in reality a neo-Marxist revolution in progress.

Despite the many obvious signs, most people in this country are still oblivious to this. Not only do they not recognize that this is an attempted revolution, the idea that it could be a Marxist one seems completely implausible. Most Americans think of Marxism as some bugaboo that is periodically brought up by wild-eyed alarmists who see a Bolshevik underneath every protest banner. They believe that this ideology has long been discredited and that no one in their right mind would take it up as a viable way of looking at the world.

In this they are only half correct. Even though it is true that history has shown Marxism to be dead wrong, Marxism is far from being dead as a worldview. Quite to the contrary, it is very much alive. It shapes – directly or indirectly – the worldview of many in the American intelligentsia, many of whom hold important posts at universities, in the media and in government.

To be sure, most of these individuals do not openly present themselves as traditional Marxists. Many of them, in fact, even concede that classical Marxism is flawed, having failed to deliver on its promises and predictions. This attitude gives these ideological mutants an air of seeming reasonableness and objectivity. But they will not let go of Marx's basic assumptions. Having retained Marx's core "insights," they either modify his theories on the edges or develop them in new directions. As a result, in the last eighty years we have witnessed a proliferation of philosophies and theoretical systems derived from Marx's teachings. Here is a partial list:

- Critical Race Theory
- The Frankfurt School
- Liberation Theology
- Critical Theory
- Black Theology
- Maoism
- The Praxis School
- De-Leonism
- Autonomism
- Austro-Marxism
- The Budapest School
- Western Marxism
- Neo-Marxism
- Structural Marxism
- Neue Marx-Lektüre
- Cultural Marxism
- Islamo-Leftism
- Trotskyism
- Left Communism
- Eurocommunism
- Freudo-Marxism
- Analytical Marxism
- Libertarian Marxism
- Marxist Feminism
- Marxist Theology
- Marxist Humanism
- Post-Marxism

Even though the theoretical systems above deal with many different aspects of the life of the individual and society, they grew from the same poisoned Marxist root. Yet despite their ignoble origin, most of these schools of thought are considered acceptable if not outright respectable.

You may have not heard of most of them, but they have exercised a deep influence in the world of ideas. These ideas have in turn influenced the way we conduct our everyday affairs. Critical race theory is one such example. This Marxist-spawned system has become the de facto worldview in many university departments, particularly in the humanities and social sciences. Astonishingly, critical race theory had been routinely taught to employees of the federal government under the guise of sensitivity training. It was only last month that President Trump, by executive order, put an end to this blatant form of Marxist indoctrination.

If you do not know what critical race theory is or where it comes from, you may find the following description illuminating:

> Critical race theory is a modern approach to social change, developed from the broader critical theory, which developed out of Marxism. Critical race theory approaches issues such as justice, racism, and inequality, with a specific intent of reforming or reshaping society. In practice, this is applied almost exclusively to the United States.[124]

Below are some of the key assumptions behind this Marxist-inspired creed:

- American government, law, culture, and society are inherently and inescapably racist.
- Everyone, even those without racist views, perpetuates racism by supporting those structures.
- The personal perception of the oppressed—their "narrative"—outweighs the actions or intents of others.
- Oppressed groups will never overcome disadvantages until the racist structures are replaced.
- Oppressor race or class groups never change out of altru-

ism; they only change for self-benefit.

- Application of laws and fundamental rights should be different based on the race or class group of the individual(s) involved.

Needless to say, the cumulative effect of all the various Marxist schools has been enormous. Slowly weaving their principles into the fabric of American life, they have gradually corroded traditional American values to the point that we are now confused about our identity. What, indeed, does America stand for? The decades-long infusion of Marxism into America's bloodstream has reached a critical level and now we are on the verge of a Marxist *coup d'état*. Find this hard to believe? Let us conduct a quick reality check.

In the last four months we have witnessed widespread "protests" and riots which shook America to the core. Serious rioting took place in hundreds of localities across the United States, causing damage and destruction unprecedented in this country's history. In a number of places chaos and lawlessness prevailed for days. Straining our system on multiple levels, these dramatic events have brought the US to the brink of breakdown. So much so that it increasingly feels as if we are slouching toward civil war.

This upheaval has been instigated by Black Lives Matter. It is this outfit that has sponsored, encouraged and organized those who have by violence driven America to the edge.

It is known that Black Lives Matter has been founded and is being run by committed Marxists. In a June article on redstate.com, the journalist Brandon Morse writes about BLM founders:

> By their own admission, their purpose isn't to heal this country, it's to rip it apart and remake it into a more Marxist kind of society... A 2015 video has resurfaced proving that the entire intent of the Black Lives Matter movement is Marxism. As you can see during the inter-

view with the Real News Network, BLM founder Patrisse Cullors admits she and her cohorts are 'trained Marxists.'[125]

BLM leaders are, in fact, quite open about their beliefs and objectives. In this video BLM co-founder Patrisse Cullors openly admits that she and her colleagues are "trained Marxists." This is what she says:

> We actually do have an ideological frame. Myself and Alicia [Alicia Garza, a co-founder of BLM] in particular, we're trained organizers. We are trained Marxists. We are super versed on ideological theories.[126]

These Marxists direct and guide the actions of BLM. It is they along with their allied groups such as Antifa – which is another Marxist outfit – who have brought this country to the precipice.

Marxism is thus not some discarded ideology harbored by a few harmless, pointy-headed professors in ivory towers. Marxism is a living creed, forming the motive behind the thinking and actions of those responsible for the present upheaval in the United States and across Western democracies. Rather than being irrelevant, Marxism is a powerful and destructive Atropic force that threatens to rip our societies apart.

The chaos has been deliberately induced, because, in order to take over, Marxists need lawlessness and disorder. When the society is destabilized and its population sufficiently confused and demoralized, the revolutionaries make their move to seize control. This can happen sooner than most people would imagine, perhaps as early as next week. If Trump should win in the upcoming election, the hard left will not accept the result and a Marxist coup may well be attempted.

STOPPING THE REVOLUTION: RESTORE LAW AND ORDER

W e argued previously that the upheaval that has been convulsing America is an attempted revolution in progress.

This revolution has been launched by American Marxists and its goal is seizure of power through the destabilization and demoralization of our communities. Once they have seized power, these Atropos- possessed revolutionaries will subvert our society by vitiating whatever traditional values and principles are still left.

We must see these events for what they are and act accordingly. It is no exaggeration to say that this is a national emergency. To prevent Marxist radicals from taking over proper measures must be taken.

The most immediate and urgent need is to restore law and order. If government has any justification at all, it is to maintain the rule of law so that its citizens are safe in their persons and property. Any government that fails to keep law and order abrogates its most basic responsibility. Such government forsakes the very duty which is given as the main reason for its existence.

No society can function successfully without the rule of law. When the rule of law is absent civil society breaks down and violence and chaos inevitably follow. Lawless societies are ripe for takeover by criminal or revolutionary elements (which are often one and the same thing). Marxist revolutionaries have always been aware of this, which is why they have sought to foment chaos and turmoil in their target countries. It is in the midst of such societal disarray that they rise to power. And after they succeed, they invariably unleash a reign of terror.

This blueprint is now being followed by Marxist revolutionists in the USA. The organization leading this effort on the ground is Black Lives Matter. BLM – along with other Marxist groups such as Antifa – constitutes the militant wing of the movement. BLM has done an excellent job as far as its mission is concerned: burning and looting on an unprecedented scale, destroying thousands of businesses, terrorizing local populations and setting dozens of cities on fire. Black Lives Matter has managed to sow chaos and lawlessness from coast to coast, inflicting a level of destruction and damage not seen in America since the Civil War.

Exploiting the disorder, the radicals have already managed to seize control in some places. It happened, for example, in Missouri's 1st Congressional District. This is the jurisdiction where Mark and Patricia McCloskey tried to defend themselves and their property from the violent BLM mob that came to terrorize their neighborhood.

As you may have heard, on June 28 BLM hooligans broke through the gate of their private community and threatened to burn their house down and kill them along with their dog. This is Mark McCloskey's description of what happened:

> Horde, absolute horde came through the now smasheddown gates coming right at the house... And these people were right up in my face, I was scared to death. And then, I stood out there. The only thing we said is 'This is private property. Go back. Private property. Leave now.' At that point, everybody got enraged. There were people wearing body armor. One person pulled

out some loaded pistol magazines and clicked them together and said that you were next. We were threatened with our lives, threatened with our house being burned down, my office building being burned down, even our dog's life being threatened. It was, it was about as bad as it can get. I mean, those you know, I really thought it was Storming the Bastille that we would be dead and the house would be burned and there was nothing we could do about it. It was a huge and frightening crowd. And there they were, at the broken gate, coming at us.[127] [transcript edited slightly for clarity]

In a truly shocking development, it was the McCloskeys who were charged with felonies in this incident while no one in the threatening mob was held to account. And this despite the fact that nine people were initially charged with trespassing (as all should have been). However, the City Council, which is run by hard-core leftists, decided to drop all charges against the so-called "protestors." Instead, the local machinery turned against the McCloskeys with a vengeance.

The campaign is led by Kimberly M. Gardner, circuit attorney for the city of St. Louis. It was she who had the obviously innocent McCloskeys indicted. People should know that Kimberly Gardner is a "Soros-funded Marxist prosecutor"[128] who works for the destruction of our society by subverting our justice system and the rule of law. In her three-year term so far as a circuit attorney, she has already let loose thousands of felons. Here is an account of her lamentable tenure from Wikipedia:

Gardner took office on January 6, 2017. She is the first African American to head the Circuit Attorney's Office. Under Gardner's tenure, St. Louis has seen a significant increase in non-prosecuted felonies. In 2019, St. Louis police sought 7,045 felony cases, but only 1,641 were prosecuted by Gardner's office. Many were returned to the police citing insufficient evidence, despite claims of sufficient evidence to prosecute by the police union.

This Marxist prosecutor is also a serious swindler and law-breaker herself. This is what we learn about her:

> In 2019, Gardner admitted to repeat campaign finance violations dating back to her time as a Missouri State Legislator. These violations included using campaign donations to pay for a private apartment. Gardner reached an agreement with the Missouri Ethics Commission to pay a settlement of $6,314 in lieu of a $63,009 fine.[129]

But the corruption of the local St. Louis judiciary is not the worst of it. One of the ringleaders of the riot at the McCloskeys' house was a woman by the name of Cori Bush. During the disturbance Bush stood in front of their residence with a bullhorn screaming "You can't stop the revolution." She was later identified by Mark McCloskey as "Marxist liberal activist leading a mob to our neighborhood."

Bush's revolutionary fervor should come as no surprise given that she is a member of the Democratic Socialists of America and other Marxist-inspired organizations. Less than two months after the McCloskey incident, Bush won the Democratic Primary in Missouri's 1st congressional district. Not surprisingly, her campaign was endorsed by Bernie Sanders, the socialist US senator from Vermont, as well other leftwing extremists. With virtually no Republican presence in the district, Bush will face no real opposition in the general election. This means that this Marxist radical will soon become a US Congresswoman from Missouri. After she is sworn into office in Washington, D.C. in January of next year, Cori Bush will join dozens of other Marxists and socialists in Congress in their pursuit of America's subversion on the federal level. According to Joshua Lawson writing in the Federalist:

> Bush will fit right in with the pre-existing "Squad" members Rep. Alexandria Ocasio-Cortez (D-N.Y.), Rep.

Ilhan Omar (D-Minn.), Rep. Ayanna Pressley (D-Mass.), and Rep. Rashida Tlaib (D-Mich.), all open socialists who were first elected in 2018.[130]

There are far more Marxists and socialists in Congress than the average voter would ever suspect. In 2014 former Congressman Allen West identified seventy such individuals.[131] Today there are many more and they are enjoying steadily increasing prominence and power. Some of the well-known figures include Bernie Sanders, Alexandria Ocasio-Cortez, Ilhan Omar, Maxine Waters, and Jerry Nadler, among many others.

Like Missouri's first Congressional district, a number of other jurisdictions in the United States are coming under the sway of Marxist radicals. As in St. Louis, they are able to use the local government, judiciary and law enforcement to pursue their agenda of dismantling of America's civil society, justice system and values. Like the Russian Bolsheviks and the Nazis just prior to their power grab, they dictate the situation on the ground through violence and intimidation. They refuse to prosecute criminals while criminalizing the actions of Americans who are trying to protect themselves from the terror unleashed by the militant arm of their Revolution.

Mark McCloskey described the situation correctly when he said:

> These radicals are not content with marching in the streets. They want to walk the hall of Congress, they want to take over, they want power... These are the people who will be in charge of your future and the future of your children.[132]

To stop this Marxist coup, it is imperative that the rule of law be restored in America. If it is not, these dangerous radicals who now control the Democrat Party and many of our institutions will use the chaos to successfully execute their power grab.

The good news is that there are enough resources on the local, state and federal levels to restore order. In those jurisdictions where this decision was taken, order was re-established within 48 hours. The reason why the lawlessness has spread is not because the law enforcement was unequal to the job, but because its hands were tied. It was simply not allowed to use the means required to stop the unrest set in motion by BLM and its supporters and collaborators. America's police have been neutralized by leftist operatives who pose as public officials. These subversives have infiltrated all levels of government and now possess sufficient clout to be able to restrain law enforcement from performing its basic duties.

The sight of cops standing by as rioting and looting is taking place is hard to take. The police have been so demoralized that, when attacked, they now routinely retreat and flee from the place of crime rather than defend themselves and the communities they are supposed to protect. Footage of mobs pouncing on abandoned police buildings and cars with impunity now proliferates everywhere.

This does not bode well. If we want to survive as a functioning society, we must let law enforcement do its job. The police must be allowed to use whatever means are necessary to put an end to the ongoing destruction of our communities. Being able to use force to stop ongoing criminal activity has always been a basic principle of policing. This principle was abandoned on May 28, 2020 when the mob attacked Minneapolis Police Department's third precinct station and Mayor Jacob Frey ordered the police to run away rather than defend the premises. Like Elvis in his heyday, the police just "left the building."

A reporter for RT documented the devastation that ensued. In a tweet she posted in the moments after the police fled, she wrote: "Police flee. Chaos utter chaos. Terrifying moment, thought I'd be hit."[133] The mayhem should have come as no surprise, since this is what generally happens when cops are ordered to abandon their posts in the face of criminal wrongdoing.

A piece titled "Precinct on Fire" which appeared at APM Reports contained the following observation:

Faced with angry, violent protesters after George Floyd's death, Minneapolis city leaders made the unprecedented decision to abandon a police station. It marked not only the further erosion of the department's relationship with the community, but perhaps the beginning of a shift in American policing.[134]

The reporter's intuition was correct: the event did mark a shift in American policing. The attitude of the Minneapolis city leaders has been adopted to various degrees by many jurisdictions across the United States. Needless to say, the results have been disastrous.

The abandonment of basic principles of law enforcement now threatens to tear apart American society. Even Joe Biden, the corrupt politician that he is, can see how things should be handled. When asked in June to comment on the upheaval that was sweeping the country, he said that "ten to fifteen percent" of Americans are "just not very good people." Many of those Joe Biden was referring to are being used as foot soldiers by their BLM Marxist organizers in the Atropic enterprise of societal destruction. Joe Biden recently elaborated how the cops should deal with such criminal elements. According to him, the police should shoot intransigent delinquents "in the leg" to stop them from committing their acts of wrongdoing if they spurn attempts at de-escalation.[135] Even though Biden's comment drew protestations from the left, which does not want to see its base risking leg injuries, the point Biden was trying to put across is in accordance with convention. It has always been the common practice to handle looters in this way. And there is a good reason for this. A society that allows looting and wanton destruction of property will sooner or later disintegrate in violence at great cost to life and everything else.

If America wants to survive as anything resembling civil society, it needs to follow the Biden protocol. Being a nation of compassion, our first concern is to prevent injury to all parties and de-escalation is obviously the preferred option. The looters should be given clear and repeated warnings, but if they choose to continue the police must be allowed to take the appropriate steps. It will be up to the looters to decide whether they wish to persist or be served the Biden medicine.

We have the moral duty and imperative to restore the rule of law in this country. If we do not do what is right, there will be a harsh price to pay. The disorder has been deliberately induced by the Marxists for the purpose of taking over our society. If we do not act, they will take advantage of the opportunity and impose tyranny and terror such as these shores have never seen.

CALLING CHOMSKY OUT: THE RIOTS ARE A FULL-FLEDGED ATTACK BY THE HARD LEFT TO TOPPLE AMERICAN SOCIETY

P rofessor Noam Chomsky, formerly of MIT, has the distinction of being the most frequently quoted academic and is arguably the best-known public intellectual in the world. He recently gave an interview in which he spoke, among other things, about the BLM sponsored riots that are taking place across the United States. This is what he had to say about them: "What's going on is a massive, non-violent, constructive social movement."[136]

As the tennis great John McEnroe used to say to wayward referees, "You cannot be serious. You just cannot be serious, sir."

Professor Chomsky has made a career of calling out lying and hypocrisy. Today we must call out his own. Below are some news items Professor Chomsky may want to read at his leisure.

From a Fox News report of June 29:

Nationwide, Floyd related protests and riots lasted 3

weeks in 140 U.S. cities, including Washington, D.C., New York; Chicago, Philadelphia and Los Angeles. By June 4 at least 40 cities in 23 states had imposed curfews. High-end boutiques in Beverly Hills and New York like Gucci and Chanel were looted, luxury stores in Santa Monica and big box retailers like Target and Macy's across the US have suffered tens of millions in losses.[137]

And this:

The costliest civil disorder in U.S. history: That's what insurance experts and city officials say the riots and demonstrations following the death of George Floyd are shaping up to be. From police overtime to losses from fire – as well as theft and other destruction – costs of the unrest are adding up. And for the first time since statistics were collected in 1950, the insurance industry has labeled this a "riot and civil disorder" catastrophe in multiple states. In Minneapolis, where some 400 businesses were damaged, owners and insurance experts estimate costs of the damage to exceed $500 million, according to the Minneapolis Star Tribune.[138]

A quote from another news item: "From police injuries to financial losses from looters, the aftermath from weeks of cross-country protests is bringing some cities to their knees."[139]

Lastly, here is an assessment of those – according to Noam Chomsky – "non-violent" and "constructive" protests by an insurance industry journal:

The civil disturbance that started in Minneapolis after the killing by police of George Floyd spread to 20 other states — an unprecedented property insurance catastrophe that will likely impact policy renewals and could even persuade some insurers to exclude coverage for damage caused by riots, executives for Verisk's Property Claim Services said. In the U.S., there has been no precedent for a riot catastrophe like this," Tom Johansmeyer, head of PCS.[140]

And should we not mention Portland which has been burning for over one hundred days running and New York City which has been essentially hollowed out?

The above reports are from weeks ago. The damage has only grown much worse since. There can be little doubt that when all is said and done the cumulative costs and losses will run into hundreds of billions of dollars. And that's if we are lucky enough not to disintegrate in the process.

This catastrophic destruction is not the work of some far-off fringe. After all, how could a small minority on the periphery wreak such immense havoc? No, this kind of violence is the thrust and focus of this destructive Atropic enterprise which is being disingenuously portrayed by the left as a "social justice" movement.

Do you want to know who is on the fringes of this campaign? They are those gullible enough to show up at the protests believing that there will be peaceful marching. These people are what Lenin used to call "useful idiots."

The real heart of this "peaceful movement" are the violent vandals who have done an excellent job indeed. They have wrecked half the country.

"Constructive" and "non-violent?" Did you really say that Professor Chomsky? What exactly is "non-violent" about all this terrible violence?

And what is "constructive" about a crusade launched under false pretenses? A sham claim is made – that the US is a racist country – and violence is let loose. This movement is not constructive: it is destructive. The whole travesty is based on a bogus allegation and conducted under false pretenses.

Since he is someone who has always portrayed himself as a scholar of complete intellectual honesty and integrity, we call upon Professor Chomsky to retract his statements about the situation on the ground which run in complete contravention of reality.

It is difficult to believe that anyone in his right mind would describe these violent riots "non-violent" and "constructive." But this is what leftists do, for they are masters of reality inversion. To listen to the leftist-speak is to enter a Twilight Zone. To them white is black and black is white. To them a violent insurrection is a gentle demonstration. To leftists a man is a woman and a woman is a man, and if you do not agree to their insanities you get cancelled and fired. And then you get threatened and you have to run for your life. This is the Left's modus operandi, which is not surprising since psychologically and ideologically they hail from the same root as tyrants and totalitarians. We have shown this in the graphic called the Ideological Pedigree Table of Values and Views.

Here is what is happening before our eyes: With America mired in a multi-prong crisis – which, sadly, is largely of our own making – the hard left has sensed that our society has been weakened to the point where it can be toppled. Taking advantage of the present weakness, the radicals are now trying to achieve their goal. From the very beginning, they have done all they could to encourage the vandals on the streets who have risen to the task by unleashing brutality that has caused heavy damage and shook America to its core. The army of wreckers have beaten and injured countless people, destroyed thousands of businesses and brought ruin to a number of cities. Rowing gangs of looters have terrorized and demoralized large swathes of the American population. The violence and chicanery have shaken this country deeply, pushing it to the brink. These domestic terrorists have been all along cheered on and protected by their enablers and shills in the media, in academia, in the courts and in the Democrat Party. What we are witnessing right now is nothing other than a full-fledged, coordinated assault against America by the armies of Atropos, the civilizational death drive. The objective of this attack is the overthrow of our society.

These are no civil rights protests to bring justice and equality to an oppressed minority. The charge of systemic institutional-ized racism against black people is completely false. The only form of institutional racism that exists in the United States is discrimination against whites and Asians in education and employment. Just recently the US Justice Department found a leading IVY League university guilty of gross discrimination against white and Asian applicants whereby such applicants had a ninety percent lower chance of being admitted than black candidates with comparable scores. From a US Department of Justice press release:

> The Department of Justice today notified Yale University of its findings that Yale illegally discriminates against Asian American and white applicants in its undergradu-ate admissions process in violation of Title VI of the 1964 Civil Rights Act. The findings are the result of a two-year investigation in response to a complaint by Asian American groups concerning Yale's conduct.[141]

If this is not racism what is, asks Patrick Buchanan in his column *The Progressive Racism of the Ivy League*. This kind of anti-white, anti-Asian racism is the common practice in academia as well as in other spheres of our societal life. The truth is that black Americans are the beneficiaries of reverse discrimination and numerous other forms of preferential treatment.

Please make no mistake. The specious charge of anti-black racism is a mere cover for unleashing violence dressed up as a "social justice movement" whose real purpose is to destabilize our society and bring about the hard left's extra-electoral coup d'état.

UTOPIA ENVISIONED: WELCOME TO THE SOCIALIST STATES OF AMERIKA

P reviously we suggested that the unfolding disarray we are witnessing in America is in reality an attempted neo-Marxist revolution. We have also spoken at some length about the important role that Black Lives Matter is playing in this process.

To obtain a realistic assessment of our predicament, however, we must be careful not to overstate the long-term significance of BLM. BLM is not the ultimate cause of our crisis. The groundwork for it had been laid long before BLM came into existence. It had been prepared in decades prior by leftists who kept systematically undermining the foundations of our society under the auspices of the Marx-inspired philosophies and ideologies.

BLM is neither the mastermind nor the originator of America's plight. BLM is merely the militant wing of America's Marxist movement, which is the primal originator of the present strife. Violent groups such as BLM and Antifa emerge into prominence when problems and contradictions in a society reach a critical point and the overthrow of the existing system becomes a realistic possibility. It is at this stage that the militants come to the fore and try to foment the maximum disarray possible. If they succeed in creating enough havoc, Marxist politicians who have infiltrated the government attempt a coup. If the system is sufficiently discomposed, the coup has a good chance of succeeding.

Although BLM is now spearheading the advancing revolution, its mission is only temporary. Should the revolution succeed, BLM's violent ways will no longer be needed. Once the Marxists seize power, there will be no more need for internal destabilization. When this comes to pass, order will be restored and BLM disbanded. Some of its more militant leaders will be cancelled (by the firing squad) and some of those who survive will be absorbed into the new ruling structures. The foot soldiers – the looters, the hooligans, the gross woke – will be sent home and told to become good socialist citizens. They will be put under discipline of hard work in order to contribute to the well-being of their new society. Their factory shifts will begin at 8:00 AM and run until 6:00 PM. They will be required to dress and behave decently, just like their counterparts in North Korea. There will be no welfare payments, pornography, drugs or rap music for them. Insolence, shouting and protesting of any kind shall not be tolerated under any circumstances. Those who refuse to submit to the new socialist rules will be quickly dealt with by the internal police. Once in their hands, the former looters and misfits will tearfully recall the old times when they were coddled by good old American cops under whose protection they enjoyed all kinds of rights. No such privileges under the new American Stasi regime! If there is a silver lining, America's Marxist revolution will put an end to sixty years of the Left's systematic destruction of the black family by misguided welfare programs. The destruction was, of course, by design because it was needed at that stage to further the Marxist agenda of subversion of American society.

Ending the moral dissolution

The new socialist regime will move quickly to enforce morality. Up until now the Marxists have used sexual dissolution as a means of unravelling America's moral fabric. They truly have done an excellent job. But it will have to stop once they are in charge. It is our prediction that a new government agency will be set up to deal with this matter. It will be called something along the lines of "The Department for Elimination of Sexual Degeneracy from the Socialist States of Amerika." If the history of other socialist regimes is any guide, transexuals will be packed off into labor camps and open homosexuals will be given the option of changing their ways or be subjected to surgical removal of their reproductive organs.

As far as racial minorities are concerned, their equality and special privileges will be quickly eliminated. No more reverse discrimination in the Socialist States of the former USA. Here is a well-known secret: socialists and leftists are inveterate racists. They have always been and they despise dark-skinned people. This attitude goes back all the way to Karl Marx who himself was a hardened and cynical racist. Marx, for example, claimed that French ethnologist Pierre Tremaux had scientifically proven that "the common Negro type is the degenerate form of a much higher one."[142]

Below is an account by Paul Kengor of the contemptible way in which Karl Marx treated his own son-in-law, Paul Lafargue, who was Cuban by birth:

> Paul came from Cuba, born in Santiago, and Marx thus viewed him as marred by 'Negro' blood and denigrated him as 'Negrillo' or 'the Gorilla.' Karl never let up his ridicule of poor Paul. In November 1882, still 14 years after Lafargue and Laura [Marx's daughter] married, Marx complained to Engels that 'Lafargue has the blemish customarily found in the negro tribe — no sense of shame, by which I mean shame about making a fool of oneself.'[143]

One wonders what the founders of BLM, who are self-confessed Marxists, think of Marx's ugly racism. Why have they not cancelled Marx given that they have cancelled others for far less egregious statements? They have, in fact, accused people of racism and subsequently done away with them for making no racist comments at all. Karl Marx, however, gets a free pass. Why is this so?

No more Black Privilege in socialist Amerika

Up to the point of their victory, American Marxists will use black people as pawns to foment racial strife and division in American society. Once they take over, blacks will lose their usefulness and the new socialist rulers will show their true colors. Black people will be scorned and treated with contempt. Now they will see and feel what real racism is. The black revolutionaries will rue their stupidity and regret bitterly that they have let themselves be duped this way. They will yearn for a return of the present America where black people enjoyed unprecedented rights and opportunities. Rather than being discriminated against, as is often falsely claimed, African Americans enjoy what amounts to Black Privilege. So efficacious is this privilege that a black person can become President of the United States even though their accomplishments are quite miniscule. Just ask Barrack Obama, a former community organizer. Had Mr. Obama been white, he would have never attained to the highest office in the land. But such is the great power of Black Privilege that it can propel black people all the way to the Oval Office despite their dearth of credentials.

There will be no more Black Privilege under the American Stasi regime, to be sure. I fully expect that not long after their victory, American Marxists will start dealing with what they will call the "Negro Question." If the history of socialist states is any guide, gulag type establishments will be set up for black people. It will not be good or pretty, but at least the duped black revolutionaries will not be able to say that they had not been forewarned. Here is the warning: don't play Marxists, because you shall be devoured by the beast.

The rich will pay for their cowardice in the socialist utopia

The rich will be another demographic to be put on the chopping block. It is truly astonishing to watch so many of them trying to play along. They think that their donations and odious virtue signaling will win them the good graces of the Atropos-possessed barbarians. An incident involving Apple shows just how spineless and pathetic some of them are. A couple of months ago, a photo appeared of an empty Apple store in one of the riot-beset cities. Knowing that the looters would likely break in, the staff had cleared out the shelves of the store. But before they evacuated, they placed a big BLM sign on the vacant table where Apple devices used to be displayed. In other words, they publicly pledged support for those who were coming to loot them and vandalize their property. Instead of taking a stand against this evil of lawlessness, theft and wanton destruction, they kiss up to the criminal elements in our society. Apple, Nike and others like them should do what is right and oppose this kind of behavior, as should every decent person and organization in America. They should demand that the police stop this criminal outrage. If the police are not able to do so, they should hire their own security to beat back the looters.

The cowardice and stupidity of the rich who run and own these woke corporations is something to behold. They believe that their pandering will get them off the hook, but in this they are badly mistaken. The rich are among the first to go after a successful leftist *coup d'état*. They are the obvious target because they have what everyone wants: wealth. In liberal democracies their property is protected by law and a web of institutions. In socialist regimes, on the other hand, there is no reliable system of property rights or protections. Wealth is freely taken from those who have it by those in power. The only way you can keep wealth in a socialist paradise is to be highly positioned in the party apparatus. (And even then your situation is precarious, since you never know when the next purge may come.) Businesspeople are never part of hard-core socialist governments, because those that rise to the top in such enterprises are usually murderers, criminals or riffraff agitators such as Stalin, Castro and Chavez. These types are naturally suspicious of practical businessfolk and harbor an instinctive dislike of them. This is why in Marxist utopias the wealthy are mercilessly cancelled (by the noose) or expropriated and exiled (the lucky ones). Despite their naïve hopes to the contrary, the same fate will befall the American rich should the unfolding revolution succeed.

Cleaning up the woke

The woke will likewise have to be dealt with promptly once the revolutionary stage ends and their usefulness is exhausted. The socialists will not want to have any clowns or oafs littering their society. Like in North Korea, all their laptops and screens shall be confiscated, and they will be duly dispatched to work. Their hair will be restored to their natural color, the rings from their noses, tongues and other body parts will be ripped away and they will be issued pretty brown uniforms in which to pass their diligent days. The screen-addicted, junk-food weaklings will be put under a vigorous exercise regime to strengthen their enfeebled bodies and minds. Under socialism we used to have massive sport events called the Spartakiads. It was a compulsory program whereby we were forced to rehearse collective athletic routines and then perform them in stadiums so that the system could show off its healthy glorious youth. The woke will greatly benefit from this kind of strict regime and their bodies and minds will be much edified in the process. After their intense sports sessions, they will have no energy or inclination to discuss their multiple gender identities.

The socialists in charge will put a quick end to all the woke nonsense, since no society – socialist or otherwise – can survive if this kind of thinking infects the minds of the population. It is truly tragic that we have not recognized this and have allowed the hard left push all kinds of perversions and inanities into the minds of our young people. A society that allows such things inevitably ends up confused and soft and becomes an easy target for a takeover. The Marxists now feel that their chance has come. The question is whether we are still capable of enough clarity and moral resolve to stop them.

LEFTISTS MUST NOT BE ALLOWED TO GET AWAY WITH THEIR CRIMINAL ELECTION FRAUD

There has been a massive and coordinated effort to steal this election from we the People of the United States of America to delegitimize and destroy votes for Donald Trump. To manufacture votes for Joe Biden. They've done it in every way imaginable, from having dead people vote in record numbers, to absolutely fraudulently creating ballots that exist only for voting for Biden.

— Sidney Powell, former Appellate Section Chief

By 10 o'clock on November 3rd, it had become apparent that Donald Trump was cruising toward a comfortable victory in the Electoral College. With Texas and Florida having gone his way, he also enjoyed sizable leads in crucial battleground states. As Trump was headed toward his seemingly inevitable victory, all of a sudden something very strange began happening. A number of key swing states in which Trump held solid margins inexplicably suspended their counts. Never in memory had a key swing state stopped its counting process before the presidential winner was known. For several states to have done this at the same time is completely unprecedented.

As the counting stretched into the days ahead and reports of gross irregularities kept pouring in, two things became obvious. First, Trump had handily won the Electoral College by legally cast ballots. Second, the Democrats were engaged in a carefully pre-planned fraud to steal the election. And the audacity of this fraud is truly unprecedented in both its effrontery and magnitude.

The Democrats' strategy going into election day should be clear to everyone by now. Their plan was to hijack the election by implementing the following stratagem:

In crucial swing and battleground states we will keep counting votes until we can accurately assess which candidate is going to win (election operatives apparently know this with near certainty when between 70-85% of cast ballots have been processed). If our candidate is on the path to win, we will simply proceed with the count and declare Biden the winner. If Biden is on a track to lose, we will suspend the count for the night. We will then proceed to manufacture ballots in the interim to enable him to win. If Trump's lead is too large, we will draw out the counting process over the next several days. As the vote drags on, we shall keep finding new votes until we have at last generated a sufficient number to put Biden over the top.

The beauty of this plan is that you do not need to exercise complete control over the electoral process in the entire state. In order to succeed, you only need to control key precincts from which you can generate enough votes to offset Trump's lead from the rest of the state. Such precincts would be located in densely populated democrat-controlled urban areas such as Atlanta, Chicago, Philadelphia, Detroit, Milwaukee and so on. These precincts had been run and controlled by the Democrat machinery for many decades. Corrupted to the core, these people have had extensive experience with election fraud on the local and state levels. This time the Democrats conspired to up their game and steal a presidential contest.

The Democratic apparatus was able to pull this scam off nearly flawlessly and things unfolded almost exactly as they had hoped. If you still have hard time believing that a national political party could be capable of such criminal malfeasance, you should listen very carefully to what Rod Blagojevich had to say the other day. You may remember that Rod Blagojevich is a former Democratic governor of Illinois who was convicted of public corruption and sentenced to 14 years in federal prison (of which he served 8). Having been part of the Democrat establishment in a swing state for many years, he knows intimately how the unscrupulous Democrat electioneering machinery works. In his interview with NewsMax, Blagojevich described exactly how the fraud took place on the night of the election day. "Coming out of the Democratic Chicago political establishment, I know how they operate," he said. He then continued: "They control polling places, they stop votes when their candidate's behind, and then in the wee hours of the morning, in the dark of night, the stealing starts."[144]

Please pay close attention to these words and ponder them carefully. We have all seen with our own eyes the abnormal sequence of events: the vote count suspended in multiple states on the night of November 3rd. Here we have a former high-level insider straight from the bowels of the corrupt Democrat apparatus telling us exactly how it happened the way it did.

Even though some fraud is part of every election, what makes this fraud extraordinary is its scope and sheer impudence. It was not just a couple of corrupt blue precincts here and there cheating in a local race. This was a synchronized operation across several battleground states to steal the highest office in the land.

But let us go back to Rod Blagojevich who had this to say about electoral fraud:

> It's a time-honored tradition in big Democrat-controlled cities like Chicago – my hometown – Philadelphia, to do precisely what they're doing now. And we've seen that in big numbers, in unprecedented numbers, in this elec-

tion in Michigan, and in Philadelphia. It's outrageous. I've never seen it on such a magnitude, because this is an indication of just how widespread it is, how deep it is, and I don't think it's confined to Philadelphia. My instincts, again, coming out of Chicago Democratic politics, my instincts tell me, it's going on in Atlanta, it's going on in Detroit, going on in Milwaukee, it's going on in Las Vegas.[145]

This colossal crime has been coordinated by various elements of the Democrat Party apparatus. There must have been cooperation between the Biden campaign and the local Democrat operatives who ran pivotal election precincts. The operation was also likely getting help and support from the Democrat National Committee and local Democratic parties in the battleground states. It would not be surprising if the effort was also aided by Deep State elements in the Federal government. It has been shown, for example, that some CIA operatives whose specialty is the orchestration of color revolutions around the world were working on behalf of the Biden campaign.

President Trump won this election. Had he not won, the Democrats would not have had to suspend the count, then drag it out until they had enough votes to declare Biden the winner. Trump should not concede to this outrage. Doing so would not only be a sellout of all those who voted for him, but it would also turn the nation over to the neo-Marxist hard left that is responsible for this travesty and whose goal is the destruction of our society as we know it.

President Trump should use all the tools and means at his disposal to try to expose this villainy. Among other things, he should order the Department of Justice and the FBI to open investigations into the matter. Individuals in these agencies resisting or sabotaging this effort must be replaced by people who are willing to carry out lawful directives of the President of the United States.

President Trump and the good people of this nation are in

the struggle of their lives. We must not let the hard left destroy this country without doing everything we can to stop the great crime they are trying to perpetrate.

MICHAEL MOORE ADMITS: THE LEFT WILL ATTEMPT A COUP

"We are all eager to join with you to repair the damage done to our country — and to eliminate that about our society and our politics which gave us Donald Trump in the first place" wrote the filmmaker Michael Moore in his open letter to Joe Biden the other day.[146]

This statement by the Oscar-winning director should put everyone on alert, because it contains a chilling revelation of the hard left's ultimate objective. Change the name "Donald Trump" for the term "*conservative*" or the phrase "*everyone who is not a leftist*" and you get an idea. Confident they have gotten a hold on the presidency, the hard left will now attempt to fundamentally alter our system in a way that would make it impossible for anyone to challenge their hold on power.

More specifically, they will seek to eliminate "that" which gives non-leftists – those who hold traditional, liberal, democratic and American values – a fair chance at electoral or legislative success. We urge you to pay careful attention to Moore's language: the Left's goal is not to try to implement their agenda through our system as it stands now. Their goal is to "eliminate" anything that may stand in their way. They do not mean to play by the rules of the game. They wish to change the parameters in a manner that would give them a permanent advantage.

Read what else Moore had to say in his missive to Joe Biden:

> I was so moved by your victory speech Saturday night when you told the immigrants and the children of immigrants that the Dreamers no longer had to live in fear. That Muslims were once again welcomed into our country. That the world could breathe a sigh of relief because we were going to let the planet Earth itself breathe and have some relief. And you told the teachers of America that starting January 20th, 'one of your own will be living in the White House.' That just felt instantly good.[147]

You can sense from the tone of Moore's letter how confident and elated the hard left feels about its prospects. Some of the measures they will try to force in their effort to permanently ensconce themselves in power include:

- Allowing unrestrained immigration from Latin America
- Mass importation of Muslims into the United States
- Elimination of the Electoral College
- Making widespread postal voting a permanent feature of America's electoral process
- Packing the Supreme Court
- Awarding Washington DC representation in US Congress
- Ending the senate filibuster
- Using teachers' unions to further speed up and deepen indoctrination of students in public schools
- Imposition of extreme environmentalist agenda such as the New Green Deal
- Blacklisting and punishing those who oppose their policies or support non-leftist candidates for office
- Destruction of the middle-class under the guise of

COVID and other purported health emergencies
- Institution of widespread political correctness through the codification of hate speech laws
- Acceleration of the LGBT agenda in public schools and institutions
- Indoctrination of government employees, contractors and recipients of federal funding through critical race theory and other Marxist-derived systems of thought

Even if they accomplish only seventy percent of their agenda, the left's hold on power will become for all practical purposes unshakeable. Thus, what they are trying to effect is nothing short of a coup, which would guarantee one Party a permanent grasp on government.

The election we just had was not yet the full coup. It was only its first stage. It is possible to have the occasional stolen election and still preserve democracy. Election theft has happened in the United States before. In the 1960 contest between Kennedy and Nixon, for example, the former was given the edge by stuffed ballot boxes from Chicago which, back then, was run by the notoriously unscrupulous mayor Richard Daley. Kennedy himself admitted so much in private. According to a piece in the American Spectator,

> [T]he day after the election, Kennedy told his friend and future Washington Post editor Ben Bradlee that Daley had told him that he had won Illinois by fraud...[148]

Despite the fraud the system was essentially preserved, because Kennedy was no far left extremist bent on radically altering the parameters of America's societal landscape.

The coup that is in the works now will have succeeded when the Left alters the system to the point when it becomes impossible to dislodge them through fair elections. As of now, they have "only" stolen an election as the first step. If Biden manages to ascend to power, they will attempt to execute their *coup d'état* in full.

If they succeed, they will try their best to preserve the appearance of democracy in America. After all, every totalitarian system has regular and "transparent" elections. In all such contests, the citizens of the afflicted country "show" their love for the Party by giving it close to one 100 percent of their vote. Only the subversives and enemies of the People display ingratitude by voting contrary to what is good for them. But then their careers (as well as their existence) are usually short-lived.

Michael Moore's open letter also reveals just how distorted leftists' view of reality is. In his cloying dispatch to Biden, he thanked him for "being a good man." To most people it has been long obvious that Joe Biden is a corrupt establishment politician who has been gaming the system for his personal benefit. The contents of his son's infamous laptop revealed just how deeply corrupt he and his family are. Here are just some of their exploits that have been reported by the New York Post:

> Hunter was getting roughly $1 million per year from Burisma. Treasury Department alerts reveal that Russian oligarch Elena Baturina wired $3.5 million to Biden's interests. New text messages reveal that China Energy Company Ltd (CEFC) apparently paid $5 million to the Biden family. Another email indicates Hunter demanded a $10 million-per-year "fee" from one of his Chinese business partners.[149]

Using his public position to enrich himself and his kin to the tune of millions of dollars, Joe Biden knows how to take care of business. Even the purportedly saintly Mrs. Biden was involved in the illicit enterprise. Holding positions in their fake companies, she helped funnel money that Joe and Hunter generated through their dirty dealings to members of their family including Joe's brother James. Astoundingly, despite Joe Biden's extensive corruption and abuse of public trust – some of which likely merits criminal convictions – Michael Moore publicly praises him as "a good man." With this being said, people of Moore's ilk are a greater danger to the future of this country than the former vice president. Driven by a revolutionary impulse, Moore is an uncompromising ideologue with a twisted moral sense. As is the case with most fierce leftists, his values are completely inverted. To him what is corrupt is good, what is good is bad and what is sacred is despicable. Just watching Moore move and speak gives one a feeling of unease. Clearly troubled but energetic and creative, people like him can wreak a great deal of damage.

Let us, then, not forget his portentous words. Let them sink in and ponder their true meaning, for the talented Mr. Moore expressed the left's plans and heartfelt desire more eloquently than anyone ever could:

> "We are all *eager* to join with you to repair the damage done to our country — and to **eliminate** <u>that</u> about our society and our politics which gave us ~~Donald Trump~~ [non-leftists] in the first place."

Thus speak totalitarians.

ABOUT THOSE 'PEACEFUL' PROTESTS: MICHELLE OBAMA AND THE DEVIOUS LEFT

O n October 7 Michelle Obama released a video statement which was pitched as her "closing message to Americans" before the upcoming November election.[150] One of the subjects she discussed were the so-called protests which have been pummeling this country for more than four months now. Amazingly, Michelle Obama described these protests as "an overwhelmingly peaceful movement for racial solidarity."

Looking straight into the camera, the former first lady claims: "It's true! Research backs it up: only a tiny fraction of the demonstrations have had any violence at all."

Michelle Obama's statement constitutes a complete denial of reality. The riots she describes as "overwhelmingly peaceful" have been anything but. Here are some facts: Thousands upon thousands of businesses have been destroyed and dozens of inner cities turned into virtual war zones. Anarchy prevailed in a number of places across the land. In Minnesota alone three hundred and sixty businesses were wrecked in the first week of the riots.[151] By the end of the second week, the damage across the United States would reach nearly two billion dollars, dwarfing the previous record set by the Los Angeles riots in 1994 ($1.42 billion in 2020 dollars). The destruction has been so extensive and widespread that the insurance industry has declared it a riot and civil unrest catastrophe in several states.

Violence erupted in most urban areas in the United States and in nearly every large city. According to a Princeton University study, riots took place in forty eight out of the fifty largest US cities.[152] In an effort to counter lawlessness, more than thirty states had to activate the national guard. More than 200 cities had to impose curfews to curb the spreading violence. There have been over fifteen thousand arrests, but this number comprises only a tiny fraction of the vandals, looters and beaters who have been terrorizing our communities. The vast majority of these delinquents will never be apprehended or persecuted for their crimes.

The reality is that the George Floyd riots have led to the most costly and destructive civil unrest in US history. In fact, our country has not seen this level of violence and devastation since the days of the Civil War.

Below we present some news items to give a flavor of this "overwhelmingly peaceful movement." From Daily Mail:

> Widespread vandalism and looting during BLM protests will cost the insurance $2 billion after violence erupted in 140 cities in the wake of George Floyd's death.[153]

From Fox Business News:

> The damage from unrest between May 26 and June 8 will be the most expensive in the nation's history, surmounting the Rodney King riots of 1992 in Los Angeles. The price tag could be as much as $2 billion and possibly more, according to Triple I. But the protests related to Floyd differ from others the database has tracked – never before have they been so widespread. 'It's not just happening in one city or state – it's all over the country,' Lor-

etta L. Worters of the Triple-I told Axios. 'And this is still happening, so the losses could be significantly more.'[154]

From Breitbart:

If you add up the insurance cost in 2020 dollars for all six major American riots during the turbulent 1960s, the total is a little shy of $1.2 billion — which means the terrorists in Antifa and Black Lives Matter caused more mayhem and property damage in a little over a week than this country saw throughout all of the 1960s.[155]

From Minneapolis Star Tribune:

More than 500 shops and restaurants in Minneapolis and St. Paul have reported damage when protests on five nights turned violent over the death of George Floyd at the hands of Minneapolis police. Dozens of properties burned to the ground. Owners and insurance experts estimate the costs of the damage could exceed $500 million.[156]

From Wikipedia:

At least 200 cities in the U.S. had imposed curfews by early June, while more than 30 states and Washington, D.C. activated over 62,000 National Guard personnel due to the mass unrest. By the end of June, at least 14,000 people had been arrested.[157]

From CNN:

Protests over the death of George Floyd raged from coast to coast – with crowds breaking curfew in major cities on another night of fury and frustrations. Fires burned and tear gas canisters flew in Minneapolis as people threw objects at officers. In Seattle, smoke filled the air as police in riot gear lined up outside stores. And in Philadelphia, firefighters doused blazes and officers chased a group of protesters down the streets for violating curfew... Looters ransacked stores on the famous Melrose Avenue in Los Angeles, leaving shelves bare and setting some buildings ablaze. The National Guard dispatched to Washington, DC, to assist police handling protests around the White House, authorities said. At least 25 cities have imposed curfews and numerous states activated National Guard forces.[158]

From the New York Times:

All Sunday night, the scene repeated itself as protesters moved through Lower Manhattan. After the main marchers would advance, fringe groups would hang back, and then the shattering glass would begin. By morning, the devastation in Manhattan was unlike anything New York had seen since the blackout of 1977. Block after block of boutiques in the Flatiron district had their windows shattered and their goods looted. All down Broadway and through the side streets of SoHo, the destruction was widespread and indiscriminate, from chain drugstores to the Chanel boutique, from the Adidas outlet to Dolce & Gabbana. Looters moved from storefront to storefront, picking through the rubble to fill garbage bags with shoes, clothes, electronics and other goods. The SoHo outpost of Bloomingdale's was ransacked.[159]

From the Washington Post:

Rioters and looters smash windows, set fires and ransack stores from Shaw to Tenleytown. ... Night of destruction across D.C. after protesters clash with police outside White House.[160]

From the Star Tribune:

In the first few days after George Floyd was killed by

Minneapolis police, rioters tore through dense stretches of Minneapolis, St. Paul and other metro communities in retaliation, causing millions in property damage to more than 1,500 locations. In their wake, vandals left a trail of smashed doors and windows, covered hundreds of boarded-up businesses with graffiti and set fire to nearly 150 buildings, with dozens burned to the ground. Pharmacies, groceries, liquor stores, tobacco shops and cell phone stores were ransacked, losing thousands of dollars in stolen merchandise. Many were looted repeatedly over consecutive nights. Other property — like gas stations, restaurants and even parked cars — was set on fire, with much of it completely destroyed. The full extent of damage to Twin Cities buildings — including residences, churches, non-profits and minority-owned businesses — could take weeks or months to calculate.[161]

The costs will be far higher and damage far more extensive than indicated by the above accounts, because the current figures are not yet available or have not been reported. All of the data on which these reports are based comes from months ago.

And yet Mrs. Obama looks you in eye and claims with a straight face that this is "an overwhelmingly peaceful movement." "It's true!" she dissembles brazenly, "research backs it up: only a tiny fraction of the demonstrations have had any violence at all."

What research? Whose research?

Even though the national media have done their best cover up the damage and destruction caused by the riots, it takes about five minutes of your research to expose Mrs. Obama's lies. Just go to duckduckgo.com and type in: "estimated cost of 2020 riots," "riots 2020 destruction," "2020 riots photos" or "videos of riots 2020."

The left's claims that the riots have been "overwhelmingly" peaceful is based on the fact that only a portion of the protestors physically engaged in actual violence. But for every actual looter there have been thirty others who incited and cheered their criminal acts. The looters and vandals do not act singly or on their own. They draw encouragement and cover from the swelling crowds around them. It is these mobs that create the energy and environment conducive for the looters and vandals to do their job. Those present in the enabling crowds are their accomplices and are guilty of criminal incitement and abetment. By engaging with and blocking the police, they also create a buffer and shield of protection for those carrying out the illicit deeds.

What Mrs. Obama calls "an overwhelmingly peaceful movement" has, in fact, been one massive juggernaut of crime, arson, assault and destruction involving hundreds of thousands of active participants and their abettors. To suggest that these louts do what they do because they aspire to "racial solidarity" or any higher ideal is an insult to the intelligence of the American people. Without any skills or prospects in life and driven to hopelessness by their undisciplined and self-indulgent lifestyles, these hooligans are there for only one purpose: destruction. Rather than falsely portraying them as some noble warriors for social justice, Mrs. Obama should call them out for the miscreants that they are. She should also point to the root cause of their lamentable condition – irresponsible parenting and forty years of ruinous liberal policies that turned our inner cities into jungles of crime, misery and despair. It is revealing that nearly every jurisdiction where serious rioting has taken place has been run for decades by Democrats.

Shortly after the release of her closing message, the actor James Woods posted on Twitter a video that showed Mrs. Obama delivering her words while, in the background, there was footage showing the destruction wrought by the rioters.[162] There is Mrs. Obama mouthing her lies while the evidence of her duplicity is projected straight behind her head for all to see. The montage is extremely effective, because it exposes Obama for the blatant liar that she is in an immediate and devastating way.

What do you think Mrs. Obama's minions did following this

exposure? Do you think they repented or apologized for her lies? No, they had James Woods cancelled and the incriminating video removed from Twitter. (The Woods' account has been subsequently reinstated. The fact that he is a famous actor and a well-known public figure probably played a role in his being able to return to the platform.)

When normal, reasonably well-adjusted people are shown the error of their views, they tend to rethink their position. But not so leftists. They instinctively double-down and go after those who expose them with their characteristic zeal and ruthlessness. Their goal is invariably the destruction of their opponents to the extent possible under the existing system. In places where leftists hold complete power, they "cancel" the objectors by disposing of them in prisons, gulags and killing fields. In nations like ours – that still possess a measure of liberty and the rule of law – they have to be satisfied with milder forms of cancellation.

The Michelle Obama incident is emblematic of leftists' modus operandi. Because their worldview is based on error and untruth, lying is their second nature. When their lies are brought to light, however, they do not renounce their falsehoods. Instead, they attack and cancel. This kind of behavior should surprise no one. We have pointed out previously how these leftists hail from the same ideological root as oppressors and totalitarians of the past.

I know this mindset well, because I grew up in the midst of it. All the hard leftists are the same no matter where they operate: they lie into your eyes and then they use violence to enforce their line. In the communist state where I grew up, they denied reality in the same shameless way that Mrs. Obama does. They claimed that the Soviet Union was the freest and most prosperous country in the world while the US was the most exploitative and oppressive. They also said that comrade Lenin was a very good and kind man while Ronald Reagan was a very bad and mean man. This was just about as true as Mrs. Obama's claims about the ongoing George Floyd's riots being "overwhelmingly peaceful." "Believe us, it is true!" they would say, "we have re-

search to back it all up."

Right.

One commentator observed that Michelle Obama is not a good actress. Indeed, she is not. She does not look authentic or genuine as she delivers her statement. To put it another way, she looks fake. And how could she not, given that she is making herself to tell lies of such magnitude. Only a person without any moral sense could look sincere doing this kind of thing. Clearly, she is not up to the task. It is sad, however, that she is trying to force herself down this path.

In her 2016 Democratic National convention speech, Michelle Obama uttered her now famous phrase: "When they go low, we go high."

Four years later in an interview with Oprah Winfrey she elaborated: "Going low is easy, which is why people go to it. It's easy to go low."[163]

It would be nice if Oprah invited Mrs. Obama for a follow-up interview and asked: Aren't you ashamed of your lies which you so impudently throw straight into people's faces? How much lower can you go?

This episode is one in many in recent months that have shown us what leftism truly is: an immoral, soul-deforming worldview. It turns people in the streets into destructive, criminal mobs and their leaders into fake lying automatons.

NOTES

---

[1] https://www.youtube.com/watch?v=3lcDT_-3v2k&feature=youtu.be&t=3536

[2] https://www.lawenforcementtoday.com/kamala-harris-about-riots-theyre-not-gonna-stop-and-they-should-not/

[3] https://www.dailysignal.com/2020/10/14/the-mob-goes-after-abraham-lincoln

[4] https://edition.cnn.com/2020/10/12/us/portland-statues-riot-trnd/index.html

[5] https://edition.cnn.com/2020/10/12/us/portland-statues-riot-trnd/index.html

[6] https://en.wikipedia.org/wiki/George_Floyd#Death

[7] https://www.express.co.uk/news/world/1292183/European-protest-Europe-Black-Lives-Matter-violence-Paris-Athens-George-Floyd-latest

[8] Ibid.

[9] https://youtu.be/kCghDx5qN4s

[10] https://blacklivesmatter.com/six-years-strong/

[11] https://www.voanews.com/europe/black-lives-matter-protests-turn-violent-across-europe

[12] Ibid.

[13] https://www.express.co.uk/news/uk/1290927/london-news-black-lives-matter-protest-violence-downing-street-george-floyd

[14] Ibid.

[15] https://blacklivesmatter.com/defundthepolice

[16] https://www.express.co.uk/news/uk/1292901/blm-protests-london-bristol-metropolitan-police-officer-injured-george-floyd

[17] Ibid.

[18] https://www.express.co.uk/news/uk/1290927/london-news-black-lives-matter-protest-violence-downing-street-george-floyd

[19] https://www.washingtonpost.com/world/europe/winston-churchill-statue-boris-johnson/2020

[20] https://www.youtube.com/watch?v=r72X5oUPTwM&t=10s

[21] https://www.unz.com/freed/a-country-not-salvageable

[22] https://www.unz.com/article/or-did-george-floyd-die-of-a-drug-overdose

[23] https://www.wsj.com/articles/the-myth-of-systemic-police-racism-11591119883

[24] https://www.thecollegefix.com/black-harvard-economist-finds-no-racial-bias-officer-involved-shootings/

[25] https://www.americanthinker.com/articles/2012/07/what_role_will_white_guilt_play_in_ the_2012_election.html

[26] https://www.wsj.com/articles/justice-department-finds-yale-discrim-

inated-based-on-race-in-undergraduate-admissions-11597351675

[27] https://www.wsj.com/articles/harvards-legal-discrimination-11570143828

[28] https://www.catholicnewsagency.com/news/cathedrals-in-6-states-damaged-by-violent-protests-91111

[29] https://www.wsj.com/articles/desecration-of-catholic-churches-across-u-s-leaves-congregations-shaken-11595451973

[30] https://www.americamagazine.org/faith/2020/07/21/jesus-statue-beheaded-catholic-churches-vandalism

[31] https://www.washingtonexaminer.com/news/churches-burned-and-vandalized-in-riots

[32] https://www.washingtontimes.com/news/2020/jul/15/black-lives-matter-protesters-turn-rage-churches-r

[33] https://www.nytimes.com/2020/06/14/us/politics/black-lives-matter-racism-donations.html

[34] https://www.washingtontimes.com/news/2020/jul/15/black-lives-matter-protesters-turn-rage-churches-r

[35] http://blog.iti.ac.at/2020/01/europe-anti-christian-attacks-reach-all-time-high-in-2019/

[36] https://youtu.be/pz-fPOjXqL4?t=425

[37] https://www.newsbreak.com/new-york/new-york/news/1579544663176/watch-kneeling-protesters-told-to-recite-revolution-is-the-solution-not-voting

[38] https://blacklivesmatter.com/now-we-transform

[39] https://www.milwaukeemag.com/milwaukees-protest-leaders-say-this-is-the-revolution/

[40] https://www.tfp.org/these-are-not-riots-but-a-revolution

[41] https://www.the74million.org/article/this-is-a-revolution-student-activists-across-the-country-take-their-place-on-the-front-lines-and-behind-the-scenes-in-historic-protests/

[42] https://www.foxnews.com/politics/ilhan-omar-dismantle-americas-economy-political-system-oppression

[43] https://www.foxnews.com/politics/george-floyd-protests-expensive-civil-disturbance-us-history

[44] http://classics.mit.edu/Aristotle/politics.5.five.html

[45] https://www.amazon.com/Black-Book-Communism-Crimes-Repression/dp/0674076087

[46] https://www.trtworld.com/sport/osaka-withdraws-from-wta-semi-final-over-police-genocide-of-black-people-39243

[47] https://www.goodreads.com/quotes/362182-truth-has-to-be-repeated-constantly-because-error-also-is

[48] https://www.wsj.com/articles/the-myth-of-systemic-police-racism-11591119883

[49] https://www.reuters.com/article/us-usa-yale-discrimination/u-s-justice-department-says-yale-illegally-discriminates-against-asians-whites-

idUSKCN2592YT

[50] https://abc7.com/nfl-black-lives-matter-blm-apology-roger-goodell-statement/6233965/

[51] https://en.wikipedia.org/wiki/Black_players_in_professional_American_football

[52] https://www.amazon.com/Black-Rednecks-and-White-Liberals-audiobook/dp/B000F3T968/

[53] https://twitter.com/hannah_natanson/status/1269742337934217219

[54] https://www.nytimes.com/video/us/politics/100000007178355/minneapolis-mayor-booed-out-of-rally.html

[55] https://www.wsj.com/articles/good-policing-saves-black-lives-11591052916

[56] https://therightscoop.com/school-principal-fired-over-honest-facebook-remarks-about-black-lives-matter

[57] https://www.thedailybeast.com/everyone-whos-been-fired-during-the-2020-racism-reckoning-from-the-times-james-bennet-to-vanderpump-rules

[58] https://www.justice.gov/opa/pr/justice-department-finds-yale-illegally-discriminates-against-asians-and-whites-undergraduate

[59] https://www.unz.com/article/or-did-george-floyd-die-of-a-drug-overdose/

[60] Ibid.

[61] https://www.politifact.com/factchecks/2020/jun/12/viral-image/bloggers-twist-history-say-democrats-wore-symbol-s/

[62] https://eu.usatoday.com/story/news/factcheck/2020/06/16/fact-check-kente-cloths-have-ties-west-african-slave-trade/5345941002/

[63] https://en.wikipedia.org/wiki/Child_sacrifice_in_Uganda

[64] https://www.africancraftsmarket.com/african-tribes/ashanti-people.html

[65] https://www.theguardian.com/commentisfree/2020/jun/07/racism-america-not-exception-norm-police-brutality-inherent-virtue

[66] https://abcnews.go.com/Politics/viruses-covid-racism-devastate-black-community-threaten-americas/story?id=71016538

[67] https://www.usatoday.com/story/news/nation/2020/06/07/black-lives-matters-police-departments-have-long-history-racism/3128167001

[68] https://therightscoop.com/must-watch-black-dc-resident-absolutely-destroys-black-lives-matter-group-from-chicago

[69] https://youtu.be/1qwif8PF1EI?t=521

[70] https://disrn.com/news/chicago-suffers-deadliest-day-in-60-years-with-18-murders-in-24-hours

[71] https://www.takimag.com/article/those-pesky-statistics/

[72] https://youtu.be/1qwif8PF1EI?t=572

[73] https://www.lewrockwell.com/lrc-blog/black-and-white-deaths-during-arrests-some-analysis/

[74]   https://thebl.com/politics/rasmussen-poll-president-trumps-approval-rating-among-black-voters-hits-all-time-high-in-the-wake-of-rioting.html

[75] https://en.wikipedia.org/wiki/African-American_family_structure

[76] https://www.fatherhood.org/father-absence-statistic

[77] https://en.wikipedia.org/wiki/The_Negro_Family:_The_Case_For_National_Action

[78] https://nypost.com/2020/01/27/barbarians-at-yale-pc-idiocy-kills-classic-art-history-class

[79] https://en.m.wikipedia.org/wiki/Human_rights

[80] https://en.wikipedia.org/wiki/Liberal_democracy

[81] https://twitter.com/benshapiro/status/1287790075439247361

[82] https://sa.org.au/interventions/gender.htm

[83] https://en.wikipedia.org/wiki/Germaine_de_Staël

[84] https://en.wikipedia.org/wiki/Rwandan_genocide

[85] https://en.wikipedia.org/wiki/Rwandan_genocide

[86] https://www.un.org/en/universal-declaration-human-rights

[87]   https://www.bostonglobe.com/opinion/2013/03/08/defense-dead-white-male-studies/PyVWxltFsjzPPzVrwF536O/story.html

[88] https://sa.org.au/interventions/gender.htm

[89]   https://www.bostonglobe.com/opinion/2013/03/08/defense-dead-white-male-studies/PyVWxltFsjzPPzVrwF536O/story.html

[90]   https://www.ibtimes.com/republican-canvasser-center-michigan-vote-count-said-she-received-death-threats-3085654

[91] https://twitter.com/votegriffin/status/1329166744431304704

[92] https://twitter.com/kylenabecker/status/1329090338984583168

[93] Ibid.

[94] https://www.youtube.com/watch?v=ipPMbE51qDM

[95] Ibid.

[96]   https://www.metrotimes.com/news-hits/archives/2020/11/18/this-man-and-his-zoom-background-emerge-as-viral-star-of-contentious-wayne-county-canvassers-vote

[97]   https://www.americanthinker.com/blog/2020/08/willie_brown_admits_it_kamala_harris_slept_her_way_to_the_top.html

[98] https://www.lawenforcementtoday.com/systematic-racism-in-policing-its-time-to-stop-the-lying

[99]   https://www.dailywire.com/news/medical-examiner-concluded-george-floyd-likely-died-of-fentanyl-overdose-court-docs-reveal

[100] https://www.lewrockwell.com/2020/11/walter-e-williams/blacks-of-yesteryear-and-today

[101]   https://justthenews.com/government/congress/democrat-compares-trump-presidency-hitler-during-holocaust-almost-hes-following

[102]   https://www.independent.co.uk/us-election-2020/trump-mussolini-putin-hitler-jim-clyburn-a9650641.html

[103] https://www.independent.co.uk/arts-entertainment/hitler-and-the-socialist-dream-1186455.html

[104] Ibid.

[105] https://www.washingtonexaminer.com/news/bernie-sanders-praised-communist-cuba-and-the-soviet-union-in-the-1980s

[106] https://eu.usatoday.com/story/opinion/2020/02/10/bernie-sanders-radical-past-donald-trump-attack-fodder-column/4706779002

[107] https://www.washingtonexaminer.com/news/bernie-sanders-praised-communist-cuba-and-the-soviet-union-in-the-1980s

[108] https://babalublog.com/2020/03/16/italian-tourist-with-coronavirus-in-cuba-exposes-the-absymal-conditions-of-the-islands-socialist-health-care

[109] https://www.foxnews.com/politics/ilhan-omar-dismantle-americas-economy-political-system-oppression

[110] https://portlandcourant.com/stories/551985086-antifa-and-blm-rioters-cheer-death-of-aaron-j-danielson-in-portland

[111] https://www.lewrockwell.com/2020/09/vasko-kohlmayer/hitler-and-the-democrats-leftwing-kindred/

[112] https://www.amazon.com/Black-Book-Communism-Crimes-Repression/dp/0674076087

[113] https://nypost.com/2020/09/26/kamala-harris-blasted-for-praising-blm-as-essential-and-brilliant-amid-violence/

[114] https://americanmind.org/features/the-racial-marxism-of-blm

[115] https://www.youtube.com/watch?v=5XxLR2r5oPg

[116] https://youtu.be/dUNe-kPnyo0?t=35

[117] https://www.nbcnews.com/politics/2016-election/meet-republicans-speaking-out-against-trump-n530696

[118] https://www.youtube.com/watch?v=TF1E0DNvhM0&feature=youtu.be

[119] https://www.thetimes.co.uk/article/bbc-films-teach-children-of-100-genders-or-more-7xfhbg97p

[120] https://news.gallup.com/poll/284285/new-high-americans-satisfied-personal-life.aspx

[121] http://www.plp.org/challenge/2020/6/12/confront-racist-cops-with-communist-discipline.html

[122] https://blacklivesmatter.com/now-we-transform

[123] https://nypost.com/2020/06/25/blm-co-founder-describes-herself-as-trained-marxist

[124] https://www.gotquestions.org/critical-race-theory.html

[125] https://redstate.com/brandon_morse/2020/06/23/black-lives-matter-marxists-n244210

[126] https://youtu.be/kCghDx5qN4s

[127] https://www.ksdk.com/article/news/local/interview-man-with-rifle-during-st-louis-protest/63-eeb61c07-4adc-4df0-a7d0-000d40a89e78

[128] https://www.americanthinker.com/blog/2020/10/

time_for_doj_to_ investigate_prosecutor_torturing_couple_who_used_guns_to_protect_their_property.html

[129] https://en.wikipedia.org/wiki/Kimberly_Gardner

[130] https://thefederalist.com/2020/09/01/meet-cori-bush-the-latest-socialist-squad-member-headed-to-congress/

[131] https://www.independentsentinel.com/heres-our-70-socialist-congressmen

[132] https://www.realclearpolitics.com/video/2020/08/24/mark_and_patricia_mccloskey_ speak_at_rnc_marxist_revolutionary_democrats_want_to_take_over_they_want_power.html

[133] https://twitter.com/SophNar0747/status/1266213127189905410

[134] https://www.apmreports.org/story/2020/06/30/what-happened-at-minneapolis-3rd-precinct

[135] https://www.youtube.com/watch?v=ZX_U59EkpeO

[136] https://www.youtube.com/watch?v=3lcDT_-3v2k&feature=youtu.be&t=3536

[137] https://www.foxnews.com/politics/george-floyd-protests-expensive-civil-disturbance-us-history

[138] Ibid.

[139] https://www.foxnews.com/us/costs-protests-financial-toll-cash-strapped-us-cities

[140] https://www.claimsjournal.com/news/national/2020/07/06/298012.htm

[141] https://www.justice.gov/opa/pr/justice-department-finds-yale-illegally-discriminates-against-asians-and-whites-undergraduate

[142] https://visiontimes.com/2020/07/10/communist-racist-how-marx-despised-blacks.htm

[143] https://www.frontpagemag.com/fpm/2020/08/so-why-not-cancel-leftist-karl-marx-paul-kengor

[144] https://www.infowars.com/posts/rod-blagojevich-democrats-committing-widespread-voter-fraud-never-seen-it-on-such-a-magnitude

[145] Ibid.

[146] https://www.hollywoodreporter.com/news/michael-moore-implores-biden-to-eliminate-electoral-college-avoid-shifting-to-cowardly-center

[147] Ibid.

[148] https://spectator.org/victory-by-fraud

[149] https://nypost.com/2020/10/24/biden-corruption-claims-all-but-confirmed-with-hunter-emails

[150] https://edition.cnn.com/2020/10/06/politics/michelle-obama-vote-joe-biden-closing-message/index.html

[151] https://www.foxnews.com/media/minnesota-newspaper-lists-over-360-local-businesses-destroyed-by-riots-with-maps-specific-details-of-damage

[152] https://www.breitbart.com/politics/2020/09/06/data-48-of-amer-

218

icas-50-largest-cities-hit-by-black-lives-matter-riots

[153]   https://www.dailymail.co.uk/news/article-8740609/Rioting-140-cities-George-Floyds-death-cost-insurance-industry-2-BILLION.html

[154]   https://www.foxbusiness.com/economy/damage-riots-1b-most-expensive

[155]   https://www.breitbart.com/politics/2020/09/16/nolte-blm-riots-are-officially-the-most-costly-manmade-damage-to-american-property-in-history

[156]   https://www.startribune.com/twin-cities-rebuilding-begins-with-donations-pressure-on-government/571075592/?refresh=true

[157] https://en.wikipedia.org/wiki/George_Floyd_protests

[158]   https://edition.cnn.com/2020/05/30/us/george-floyd-protests-saturday/index.html

[159]   https://www.nytimes.com/2020/06/01/nyregion/nyc-looting-protests.html

[160]   https://www.washingtonpost.com/gdpr-consent/?next_url=https%3a%2f%2fwww.washingtonpost.com%2flocal%2fdc-braces-for-third-day-of-protests-and-clashes-over-death-of-george-floyd_story.html

[161]   https://www.startribune.com/minneapolis-st-paul-buildings-are-damaged-looted-after-george-floyd-protests-riots/569930671

[162]   https://twitter.com/RealJamesWoods/status/1313924275246493697

[163]   https://www.cnbc.com/2020/02/12/michelle-obama-on-famous-catchphrase-when-they-go-low-we-go-high.html

Made in the USA
Coppell, TX
05 November 2021